MW00990949

THE
HIGH-PROTEIN
VEGAN
COOKBOOK

Also by Ginny Kay McMeans

The Make Ahead Vegan Cookbook

THE
HIGH-PROTEIN
VEGAN
COOKBOOK

125+ HEARTY PLANT-BASED RECIPES

Ginny Kay McMeans

The Countryman Press
A division of W. W. Norton & Company
Independent Publishers Since 1923

Copyright © 2019 Ginny Kay McMeans

All rights reserved
Printed in China

For information about permission to reproduce selections from this book, write to
Permissions, The Countryman Press, 500 Fifth Avenue, New York, NY 10110

For information about special discounts for bulk purchases, please contact
W. W. Norton Special Sales at specialsales@wwnorton.com or 800-233-4830

Manufacturing through Asia Pacific Offset
Book design by LeAnna Weller Smith
Production manager: Devon Zahn

The Countryman Press
www.countrymanpress.com

A division of W. W. Norton & Company, Inc.
500 Fifth Avenue, New York, NY 10110
www.wwnorton.com

978-1-68268-259-3

10 9 8 7 6 5 4 3 2 1

Dedicated to each and every member of my family. All 104 of them. They have always supported me with love and encouragement.

CONTENTS

New ingredients, techniques, and even small appliances add up to my happiness in the kitchen. It was so exciting when I turned to vegan cooking and found a whole new world of products. This adventure was all the more fun because I had to make sure that nutrients and minerals were well represented. It turned out that it wasn't very hard to do. Eating a variety of food throughout the day made nutrition just fall into place. Finding protein powerhouses like seitan, tofu, and tempeh was an added bonus.

As a food blogger, one major question I get from vegans is how they can get enough protein in their diets. My quick answer is to make sure to eat a variety of food in all the colors of the rainbow. This cookbook, *The High-Protein Vegan Cookbook*, is my long answer. The recipes in this book cover every aspect of the day, with an emphasis on including a high protein count in every recipe.

I'm so glad you are here. Pick your chapter and let's get cooking.

WHAT PROTEIN IS AND WHY WE NEED IT

It's easy to maintain a healthy and fit body with a plant-based diet, even when you're intent on building muscle. This cookbook is here to show you how easy that is—each and every recipe features ingredients that serve you multiple grams of protein.

There is a myth floating around that meat, eggs, and dairy products are the be-all and end-all for protein. Not true. For instance, 1 cup of peas contains 8 grams of protein, 1 cup of cooked spinach has 7 grams, and 1 cup of quinoa has 8 grams. In other words, it's easy to get enough protein in your diet with beans, nuts, seeds, greens, soy, and grains.

Protein helps the body digest food and it also makes us feel full longer. When you hear someone saying they feel hungry all the time, it means they probably aren't getting enough protein. Protein also helps a body grow, helps build all the tissues in the body, helps repair that tissue, and so much more. We must have protein.

Here is some science made easy: Proteins are made up of amino acids. Of the hundreds of amino acids, only twenty make up protein. Our bodies automatically produce these amino acids except for nine essential amino acids that must be supplied to us through food.

A complete protein has all of the nine essential amino acids. Given the varied types of food that vegans eat, that is not hard to find at all. For instance, a peanut butter sandwich on whole wheat bread is a complete protein. In fact, combine any legume with a grain and you have a complete protein. Hummus and pita? Yes! There are also a few stand-alone complete proteins in the plant kingdom. Buckwheat, soy (tofu, tempeh, edamame), hempseed, and quinoa are complete proteins in themselves.

Now let's go one step further. The good news is we don't have to worry about pairing proteins at a single meal. As long you ingest each of the nine essential amino acids during the day, then you will receive what is considered to be a complete protein. So instead of peanut butter on toast at one meal you can have toast in the morning and Thai peanut butter sauce that evening. But, hey! If you'd like to have a bean and rice burrito, go for it. There's nothing wrong with getting a complete protein in one sitting.

HOW MUCH PROTEIN DO WE NEED?

How many grams of protein do we need in a day? For a woman it's 0.5 to 1 gram per pound that you weigh. It varies between studies, but this range appears in most. Luckily, it's not hard to acquire. So a 130-pound woman needs 65 grams of protein in a day to maintain a balanced diet. If she is trying to build muscle, then she should aim for 130 grams per day.

A man's protein intake should be 0.8 to 1.5 grams per pound that he weighs. So a 175-pound man should get 140 grams, and 263 grams if he is trying to really bulk up. Bodybuilders and pro athletes often add protein supplements on top of protein-rich diets. While some protein powders are meat- or dairy-based, vegans only use protein powders that are dairy free (such as pea protein).

It's better for your body to process a divided amount of

protein throughout the day instead of all at once. So, for instance, a seitan burger plus a protein shake in one sitting isn't going to provide you with the actual protein contained in those foods. Your body will process whatever you feed it, but it will not always do so optimally. The ballpark amount of protein that your body will use at one time is 30 grams. It takes a couple of hours for your body to process that protein. This is the rhythm in which we usually eat anyway, so getting enough protein is pretty much a no-brainer.

If you're bodybuilding or an athlete, then you need to check your own numbers, because you would require more than usual for meals and snacking. A scoop of protein powder once or twice a day is an easy way to make sure you've added the extra protein you need without stuffing yourself.

As always, drink plenty of water.

SEITAN, TOFU, AND TEMPEH!

Seitan, tofu, and tempeh are protein powerhouses of the vegan world. A little goes a long way in terms of protein and satisfaction. All three products start with vegetables or grains and have been used by cooks for hundreds of years. You can recreate most of your childhood favorites and cherished comfort foods by using one of these ingredients.

LET'S TALK SEITAN

Seitan is a plant-based product that is made from grains and vegetables. The result of this combination is a textured product that can be sliced, diced, pulsed, and chopped. You can even shape it before cooking into any form, including nuggets or patties. It can be tender and it can be chewy. It's all in the mix and kneading.

Seitan can be bought premade or it can be made at home. Store-bought seitan isn't always marked as such, so you need to look at the ingredients. If the first ingredient is vital wheat gluten, then it is seitan. Be on the lookout for additives and preservatives. As always, making your food from scratch is the best way to really know what you're eating.

Since seitan can be easily made at home, and because it also results in a great product, my vote goes to homemade seitan. It all starts with vital wheat gluten, which is a flour that is

70–80 percent protein. You can buy non-GMO versions, so that's another plus. Ingredients are added for flavor, and then all is cooked low and slow.

Not only do you get a great boost of protein with seitan, you also get fabulous texture and flavor added to your recipes. Plus, it's economical. One pound of raw dough turns into about 2 pounds of cooked seitan. Including all ingredients, that is close to only $2.00 for 2 pounds of a delicious textured product that you can slice for sandwiches, cube into casseroles, crumble into tacos, have as a main course, and so much more.

The last chapter of this book is titled "Let's Make Seitan." You'll find multiple recipes with different flavors and cooking methods. I have made these recipes over and over again, and they are fail proof.

TOFU IS VERSATILE

Tofu is a tasteless soybean product that's been around almost 2,000 years. True, it didn't appear in our grocery stores until the 1950s, but it had been completely explored a very long time before that. The love of tofu escaped many of us until recent years, but it has finally become a beloved ingredient. Tofu is made in two forms: silken and regular, and it is high in protein, low in cost, and versatile in recipes. Tofu is some darn good stuff.

Silken tofu comes as a silky mass that adds so much to puddings and desserts and even some types of soup. Silken tofu is undrained and unpressed, and it comes in soft, firm, and extra-firm versions. The version is clearly marked on the package. Even extra-firm silken tofu has a creamy texture.

Tofu that is not silken is called regular tofu and is found in the refrigerated section in grocery stores. Regular tofu is best when it is drained and pressed. And if it is marinated, it will take on the flavor of the marinade.

Silken tofu needs to be drained and/or patted dry. Soft block regular tofu needs to be drained, and medium, firm, and extra-firm tofu need to be drained and pressed. All recipes in this book will state which type of tofu you need and how to prepare it.

If tofu is new to you, then a great introduction to this ingredient is scrambled tofu. You can add so many things to scrambled tofu, and it makes for a filling and high-protein breakfast with very little effort. Tofu can also be prepared so that it's crispy on the outside and softly textured on the inside. For example, see the recipe Fried Hoisin Tofu with Peanut Sauce—

Touched Udon (page 271). Marinating tofu is a very easy way to add more flavor to it, and marinated tofu gives *oomph* to a dish. At the far extreme, silken tofu can be used in high-protein treats such as puddings and shakes.

HOW TO PRESS TOFU

There are several ways to press tofu. First open the package and drain away the water. Then stack many paper towels on a dinner plate. Place the tofu on the paper towels and add more paper towels on top of the tofu. Put another plate on top of those towels. Now weigh it down with cans or an iron skillet. The paper towels will soak up the liquid as it is being pressed. Alternately, you can buy a tofu press. The one I have lets you slide your tofu between two hard layers and then there are two latch screws that you tighten. Set the press on its side on a plate and let it drain the liquid from the tofu. This takes about 10 to 20 minutes.

TEMPEH, A LITTLE SOMETHING EXTRA

Tempeh is also made from soybeans, but it is different from tofu in many ways. Tempeh is made from cooked and fermented soybeans and is very firm but not hard. It has a unique taste but also can be marinated. Tempeh can be sliced extremely thin or cut into small blocks.

Flavored tempeh products are also available in grocery stores. You can try these and see what you think, but if you buy "original" versions of tempeh you can control the seasonings and flavors. Since tempeh is so easy to cut into any form, you can slide it into just about anything.

TOP VEGAN SOURCES FOR PROTEIN

All nuts, grains, vegetables, fruit, and seeds have protein. Here is a list of some ingredients that rank highest in protein.

VEGETABLES AND BEANS	SERVING SIZE	PROTEIN
Alfalfa Sprouts	½ cup	14 grams
Artichoke Hearts	½ cup	4 grams
Asparagus	1 cup	3 grams
Black Beans	½ cup	8 grams
Black-Eyed Peas	½ cup	8 grams
Broccoli	1 cup	4 grams
Brussels Sprouts	1 cup	3 grams
Chickpeas	½ cup	7 grams
Corn	1 cup	4 grams
Edamame	½ cup	8 grams
Green Beans	1 cup	8 grams
Kale, uncooked	1 cup	4 grams
Kidney Beans	1/2 cup	8 grams
Lentils, cooked	½ cup	9 grams
Mushrooms, uncooked	1 cup	4 grams
Peas	1 cup	8 grams
Pinto Beans	1/2 cup	8 grams
Potatoes	1 cup	4 grams
Soy Milk	1 cup	8 grams
Spinach, uncooked	1 cup	5 grams
Sun-Dried Tomatoes	1/2 cup	3 grams
Sweet Potato	1 cup	5 grams
Tempeh	1/2 cup	10 grams
Tofu	1/2 cup	10 grams
TVP (Textured Vegetable Protein), cooked	¼ cup	11 grams

GRAINS	SERVING SIZE	PROTEIN
Amaranth	1 cup	7 grams
Buckwheat, uncooked	1 cup	6 grams
Oats, uncooked	1 cup	6 grams
Seitan, cooked	1 cup	30 grams
Sprouted Grain Bread	2 slices	10 grams
Teff	1 cup	14 grams
Wild Rice, cooked	1 cup	7 grams
SEEDS AND NUTS	**SERVING SIZE**	**PROTEIN**
Almond Butter	2 tablespoons	7 grams
Almonds	1 cup	7 grams
Cashews	1/4 cup	10 grams
Chia Seeds	2 tablespoons	5 grams
Hemp Milk	1 cup	5 grams
Hempseed	2 tablespoons	8 grams
Peanut Butter	2 tablespoons	8 grams
Peanuts	¼ cup	9 grams
Pepitas (pumpkin seeds)	¼ cup	8 grams
Pistachios	¼ cup	6 grams
Quinoa	1 cup	8 grams
Tahini	2 tablespoons	8 grams
Walnuts	1/2 cup	6 grams
ADDITIONS	**SERVING SIZE**	**PROTEIN**
Nutritional Yeast	2 tablespoons	8 grams
Spirulina	2 tablespoons	4 grams

So let's get started with some satisfying, high-protein recipes that will help keep you going throughout the day while keeping you strong and healthy.

CHAPTER ONE

POWER-UP
APPETIZERS

BROCCOLI VEGGIE DIPPERS

YIELD: 6 SERVINGS

Get your vegetables the fun way. These dippers are small patties that you can pick up with your fingers. Eat them plain or dip them into your favorite sauce. Party food!

INGREDIENTS:

- ¾ cup lentils
- 2 cups broccoli florets, fresh
- 1 tablespoon ground chia seeds
- ½ cup shredded carrots
- ¼ teaspoon garlic powder
- ¼ teaspoon dried parsley
- ½ teaspoon salt
- ¼ teaspoon ground black pepper
- ¼ teaspoon onion powder
- ¼ teaspoon dried oregano
- ¼ teaspoon dried basil
- ¾ cup breadcrumbs, divided
- 1 tablespoon extra virgin olive oil

INSTRUCTIONS:

1. Rinse and drain the lentils. Place the lentils in a medium-large saucepan. Pour in ½ cup water. Place the pan on high heat and bring to a boil. When the water comes to a boil, turn down to medium high and cook for 20 minutes or until the lentils are tender. All the water should be absorbed. Set aside.

2. Meanwhile, add water to a medium saucepan with a steamer insert and bring to a boil. Add the broccoli to the insert and steam over boiling water for 10 minutes. Remove from steamer and set aside.

3. Mix ground chia seeds with 3 tablespoons water in a small bowl.

4. Place all ingredients in a food processor, except ¼ cup breadcrumbs. Process until well combined, with a crumbly texture. Divide mixture into twelve pieces. Roll each piece into a ball and then flatten them into patties. Coat each patty, on each side, with the remaining breadcrumbs.

5. Heat the oil in a medium skillet to medium high and brown the patties for 3 minutes on each side.

6. Serve with dairy-free chipotle mayonnaise or any of your other favorite spicy dipping sauces.

Protein: 6 grams per serving (2 patties)
Active Time: 10 minutes
Cook Time: 25 minutes
Total Time: 35 minutes

RAINBOW VEGGIE PROTEIN PINWHEELS

YIELD: 6 SERVINGS

Julienned vegetables are laid across a bed of hummus and crumbled tempeh, and then all are wrapped up in the perfect holder: a green spinach tortilla. Even the pickiest of eaters will want to have one.

INGREDIENTS:

¼ cup hummus

¼ cup tempeh, crumbled in a food processor

2 large spinach tortillas

¼ cup thinly sliced red bell pepper

¼ cup thinly sliced yellow bell pepper

1 carrot, sliced thin

¼ cup very thinly sliced purple cabbage

INSTRUCTIONS:

1. Mix together the hummus and tempeh.

2. Lay out tortillas. Spread hummus mixture in a thin layer over the whole surface of each tortilla stopping 1 inch from the edges. Lay a thin strip of each of the four vegetables, next to each other, over the hummus mixture.

3. Roll each tortilla tightly and cut crosswise into pinwheels. You can use toothpicks if needed, but the hummus helps them stick together at the edges.

Protein: 9 grams per serving (2 pinwheels)
Active Time: 20 minutes
Total Time: 20 minutes

TEMPEH CHICKPEA STUFFED MINI PEPPERS

YIELD: 6 SERVINGS

Colorful mini bell peppers wrap these protein-packed appetizers into pretty little packages. Chickpeas and tempeh are just the start of a flavorful mix.

INGREDIENTS:

12 ounces multi-colored sweet mini peppers

2 15-ounce cans chickpeas, drained and rinsed

¾ cup tempeh, chopped

½ cup dairy-free mayonnaise

¼ cup cider vinegar

1 teaspoon ground mustard

3 scallions, thinly sliced

1 teaspoon salt

¼ teaspoon cayenne pepper

INSTRUCTIONS:

1. Cut off the stem end of the peppers. Slice lengthwise. Remove any seeds that are inside. Set aside.

2. Place all the remaining ingredients in a food processor. Pulse four or five times. The chickpeas should be chunky. Remove the blade and stir to make sure the mixture is blended well.

3. Stuff each pepper half full with about 2 tablespoons of the chickpea mixture. Set on a plate to serve.

Protein: 9 grams per serving (2 mini peppers)
Active Time: 20 minutes
Total Time: 20 minutes

PROTEIN POWER GRILLED VEGGIE AND FRUIT SKEWERS

YIELD: 4 SERVINGS

We've all heard of fruit skewers, but have you heard of fruit and marinated tofu skewers? All are grilled on a stick to make the prettiest and freshest finger food around.

INGREDIENTS:

8   ounces extra-firm tofu, drained, pressed (page 17), and cut into 1-inch cubes

2   tablespoons tamari

1   tablespoon rice vinegar

1   tablespoon maple syrup

¼   teaspoon chili powder

1   large sweet potato, peeled and chopped into bite-size chunks

4   ounces cremini mushrooms

1   pineapple, chopped into chunks

1   red bell pepper, chopped into large pieces

1   yellow bell pepper, chopped into large pieces

Extra virgin olive oil, for grilling

INSTRUCTIONS:

1. Place the tofu cubes in a large bowl. In a small bowl, mix the tamari, rice vinegar, maple syrup, and chili powder together and pour over tofu. Marinate for 30 minutes.

2. Parboil the sweet potato chunks for 10 minutes or until just tender.

3. Clean the mushrooms and cut off the ends of the stems. If some of the mushrooms are large, cut into halves or thirds.

4. Skewer the tofu, sweet potato, pineapple, red and yellow bell peppers, and mushrooms onto each skewer.

5. Brush grill or grill pan with oil and set to medium-high heat. Grill skewered vegetables and fruit until there are grill marks. Flip and grill the other side.

Protein: 16 grams per serving (2 skewers)
Active Time: 15 minutes
Cook Time: 25 minutes
Total Time: 40 minutes

CHICKPEA SALAD CROSTINI

YIELD: 6 SERVINGS

This appetizer starts with fresh toasted Italian bread slices. Top that off with spicy citrus marinated veggies and you have a winning finger food.

INGREDIENTS:

1   baguette, cut into 12 slices

2   tablespoons extra virgin olive oil

1   15-ounce can chickpeas, drained and rinsed

1   15-ounce can black beans, drained and rinsed

1   8-ounce can corn, drained and rinsed

1   4-ounce can black olives, drained and sliced

1   tablespoon fresh lime juice

2   teaspoons flaxseed meal

1   teaspoon ground cumin

¼   teaspoon chili powder

¼   teaspoon onion powder

¼   teaspoon salt

Fresh thyme, for garnish

INSTRUCTIONS:

Crostini Toasts

1. Lay out the bread slices on a baking sheet. Lightly brush each slice of bread with oil. (The new silicone brushes are great for this, and they wash up really easily.) Put the baking sheet under the broiler. Don't do anything else. Just stand there and keep checking the bread and don't let it burn. It only takes a couple of minutes. After the toasts are lightly browned, remove the sheet from the oven. You can make these ahead of time and keep them in the refrigerator for later use, too.

To Assemble

2. In a large bowl, mix all the remaining ingredients together, except the thyme.

3. Top each toast with the chickpea mixture just before serving. Garnish with fresh thyme.

Protein: 8½ grams per serving (2 crostini)
Active Time: 15 minutes
Cook Time: 5 minutes
Total Time: 20 minutes

THAI SWEET CHILI TOFU STACKS

YIELD: 6 SERVINGS

In preparation for a party, make your life easier by using some prepackaged ingredients. You and your guests will love these beautiful skewers of marinated tofu, with lots of flavor in each bite.

INGREDIENTS:

1   tablespoon cornstarch

½   cup rice vinegar

½   cup coconut sugar

1   chili pepper, such as jalapeño or cayenne, chopped fine

2   cloves garlic, chopped fine

2   teaspoons tamari

½   teaspoon chopped parsley

¼   teaspoon cayenne pepper

8   ounces extra-firm tofu, drained, pressed (page 17), and cut into 1-inch cubes

1   8-ounce can sliced pineapple

INSTRUCTIONS:

1. Prepare the sauce by mixing the cornstarch and 1 tablespoon of water together until smooth and set aside.

2. Add the rice vinegar, ⅔ cup water, sugar, chili pepper, garlic, tamari, parsley, and cayenne pepper to a food processor. Process until well blended and the chili pepper is broken up very well.

3. Pour mixture into a small saucepan and heat until boiling, stirring until the sugar is dissolved. Turn down heat and cook 5 minutes. Add the cornstarch mixture and stir occasionally for about 5 minutes or until mixture is a bit thickened. Take off heat and let it cool.

4. Add the tofu cubes to the cooled sweet chili sauce. Let marinate about 30 minutes.

5. Drain the pineapple and slice the rings into about 1- to 1¼-inch wedges.

6. Place a slice of pineapple on a plate and center a cube of marinated tofu on top. Place another slice of pineapple on the tofu and secure with a toothpick.

Protein: 9 grams per serving (4 stacks)
Active Time: 30 minutes
Cook Time: 15 minutes
Total Time: 45 minutes

SPICY CHICKPEA SEITAN TOFU ROLLUPS

YIELD: 6 SERVINGS

A super simple process and easy handling are two pluses for these protein-rich rollups. Tofu mingles with tasty ingredients to make for a great base.

INGREDIENTS:

2 ounces extra-firm tofu, drained and pressed (page 17)

1 cup canned chickpeas, drained and rinsed

2 tablespoons dairy-free chipotle mayonnaise

1 tablespoon hot sauce

2 teaspoons hempseed, toasted in shell

2 teaspoons tahini

½ teaspoon cider vinegar

½ teaspoon garlic powder

1 green onion, chopped

¼ teaspoon salt

Pinch of ground black pepper

½ cup Steamed Seitan Smoky Nuggets (page 283)

2 large spinach tortillas

Fresh parsley, for garnish (optional)

INSTRUCTIONS:

1. Add the tofu, chickpeas, mayonnaise, hot sauce, hempseed, tahini, vinegar, garlic powder, onion, salt, and pepper to a food processor. Process until well combined and spreadable with a knife.

2. Chop seitan nuggets into very small pieces. (You could also pulse in a food processor a couple of times.) Fry seitan in a small skillet over medium-high heat for about 4 minutes, stirring often to keep from burning. Set aside.

3. Divide the tofu filling into two portions and spread evenly onto each tortilla. Leave about an inch from the edge on one side without filling to aid in rolling. Sprinkle seitan over each tortilla. Start rolling each tortilla at the opposite side of the edge that you did not cover. Roll firmly but not too tight, so as not to squeeze out the filling.

4. Pin toothpicks along the edge of the tortilla about 1½ to 2 inches apart. Slice between each toothpick. This helps to keep the rolls together until you can set them on a plate. They do stick together very well. Garnish with fresh parsley, if desired.

Protein: 11 grams per serving (2 rollups)
Active Time: 20 minutes
Cook Time: 5 minutes
Total Time: 25 minutes

CUCUMBER SEITAN ROLLUPS

YIELD: 6 SERVINGS

Everyone will want to pick up one of these pretty little rolls of veggies and protein. Pop one in your mouth and enjoy the flavors and textures.

INGREDIENTS:

1   red bell pepper

1   orange bell pepper

1   yellow bell pepper

2   6-inch cucumbers

¼   cup hummus

¼   teaspoon salt

¼   teaspoon ground black pepper

⅓   cup seitan, crumbled (Slow Cooker Log for Thin Slices and Crumbles, page 280)

INSTRUCTIONS:

1. Slice the bell peppers until you have eighteen thin toothpick-size strips of each color, and then chop the remaining peppers into a very fine dice (should be at least 3 tablespoons of each color; you may have some leftover). Set aside.

2. Use a vegetable peeler to slice off long strips from the cucumbers. Keep the same direction so that some green will be on each long edge of the strips. Slice on all four sides and discard the center seed section. You will have about two or three slices from each of the four sides of the cucumber.

3. Lay out the slices. Spread about 2 teaspoons hummus down the center of each strip; spread out evenly, keeping a little bit away from the long edge. Sprinkle a dash of salt and pepper on each hummus-covered cucumber. Now sprinkle about 1½ teaspoons each of seitan and chopped bell pepper mix on each slice.

4. Roll up each cucumber and secure with a tooth-pick. Set on their sides and slide three different-colored bell pepper strips into the center at different heights. You will need to cut some of them shorter to achieve this look.

Protein: 6 grams per serving (2 rollups)
Active Time: 15 minutes
Cook Time: 15 minutes
Total Time: 30 minutes

LENTIL BALLS IN SWEET AND SPICY RED SAUCE

YIELD: 6 SERVINGS

A crispy lentil bean ball gets mixed into a tangy tomato sauce for this appetizer. Make sure to have napkins and toothpicks on hand, but you'll have no need for a leftover container.

INGREDIENTS:

Lentil Balls

¾ cup green lentils

1½ cups vegetable broth

2 teaspoons extra virgin olive oil

⅓ cup diced onion

⅓ cup quick-cooking oats

⅔ cup grated carrots

2 cloves garlic, finely chopped

2 tablespoons tomato paste

1 tablespoon aquafaba

¾ teaspoon Italian seasoning

¾ teaspoon salt

Pinch of ground black pepper

INSTRUCTIONS:

Lentil Balls

1. Rinse and drain the lentils. Place lentils in a medium-large saucepan. Pour in the vegetable broth and cover. Place pan on high heat and bring to a boil. When boiling, turn down to medium high and cook for 20 minutes or until the lentils are tender. All the water should be absorbed. This process can also be done in a rice cooker.

2. Preheat the oven to 425°F.

3. Heat the oil in a small skillet over medium-high heat. Add the onion and sauté until translucent, about 10 to 15 minutes.

4. Add the cooked lentils, sautéed onions, oats, carrots, garlic, tomato paste, aquafaba, Italian seasoning, salt, and pepper to a large bowl. Mix very well.

5. Roll pieces of the lentil mixture into eighteen balls and place on a baking sheet. Bake for 10 minutes, then flip, and bake another 10 minutes.

Protein: 12 grams per serving (3 lentil balls)
Active Time: 20 minutes
Cook Time: 45 minutes
Total Time: 1 hour 5 minutes

The High-Protein Vegan Cookbook

Sweet and Spicy Sauce

¼ cup diced onion

1 15-ounce can fire-roasted tomatoes

½ cup ketchup

3 tablespoons Tabasco

½ cup crushed pineapple

2 tablespoons cider vinegar

2 tablespoons maple syrup

½ teaspoon salt

½ teaspoon ground black pepper

Sweet and Spicy Sauce

6. Add all the sauce ingredients to a food processor. Blend well until almost smooth. There should still be small pieces of pineapple.

7. Pour into a large saucepan. Bring to a boil then turn down to medium heat.

8. Carefully add lentil balls to the pan and fold them into the sauce. Heat through about 5 minutes and then serve with toothpicks.

CHICKPEA BALL POPPERS

YIELD: 6 SERVINGS

There are so many tasty ingredients wrapped up in these little balls. Not only that! There's also a spicy vegan mayo dip to go right alongside.

INGREDIENTS:

Chickpea Balls

1   28-ounce can chickpeas, drained (save the liquid to use as aquafaba) and rinsed

1   teaspoon tamari

2   teaspoons onion powder

1   teaspoon salt

½   teaspoon ground black pepper

4   tablespoons aquafaba

1   cup fresh breadcrumbs

Spicy Mayo Dip

½   cup vegan mayonnaise

¼   cup sweet chili sauce

1   teaspoon tamari

½   teaspoon Tabasco

INSTRUCTIONS:

Chickpea Balls

1. Preheat the oven to 400°F.

2. Add all the chickpea ball ingredients to a food processor. Pulse until the chickpeas are broken down and the ingredients are mixed. Form mixture into twenty-four bean balls and place them on a baking sheet. Bake for 25 minutes.

Spicy Mayo Dip

3. Mix all the dip ingredients together thoroughly.

4. Serve in a bowl with toothpicks alongside the chickpea ball poppers.

Protein: 10 grams per serving (4 ball poppers)
Active Time: 15 minutes
Cook Time: 25 minutes
Total Time: 40 minutes

ENGLISH MUFFIN PROTEIN TRIANGLES

YIELD: 6 SERVINGS

Here's a unique appetizer that's easy to make. Flavor-packed ingredients are blended together and piled high on English muffins. After broiling and slicing, you have bite-size treats that you'll want to serve again and again.

INGREDIENTS:

3   English muffins

⅔   cup raw almonds, soaked in water from one hour to overnight

1½ tablespoons lemon juice

1½ tablespoons nutritional yeast

1   teaspoon curry powder

½   teaspoon mustard powder

½   teaspoon salt

Pinch of ground black pepper

⅓   cup extra virgin olive oil, more if desired

⅓   cup seitan, crumbled (Slow Cooker Log for Thin Slices and Crumbles, page 280)

¼   cup black olives, sliced

Freshly cut parsley, for garnish (optional)

INSTRUCTIONS:

1. Break apart the English muffins at the center and toast. Place on a baking sheet and set aside.

2. Place the almonds in a food processor. Add lemon juice, nutritional yeast, curry powder, mustard powder, salt, and pepper. Blend until the mixture is as smooth as you can get it. It will still have a few little pieces. Slowly pour in the olive oil through the opening in the lid. You may add a little more oil if you would like it thinner. Pour mixture into a small bowl and mix with the crumbled seitan.

3. Divide the mixture and spread on the six muffin halves. It will be thick. Slide the baking sheet under the broiler for about 2 minutes, until lightly golden.

4. Top with black olive slices and cut each muffin into quarters. The easiest way to do this is by using a cleaver and pushing straight down as you would cut pizza. Stack on a plate and garnish with freshly cut parsley, if desired.

Protein: 12 grams per serving (4 triangles)
Soaking Time: 1 hour
Active Time: 20 minutes
Cook Time: 2 minutes
Total Time: 1 hour 20 minutes

The High-Protein Vegan Cookbook

CRISPY BAKED PUFFED TOFU WITH TERIYAKI SAUCE

YIELD: 6 SERVINGS

Puffed tofu is a fun way to enjoy tofu. Seasoned and baked, the result is crispy on the outside and creamy on the inside.

INGREDIENTS:

Puffed Tofu

7 ounces extra-firm tofu, drained and pressed (page 17)

½ cup vegetable broth

2 tablespoons hot sauce (such as Frank's)

¼ cup cornstarch

Dipping Sauce

2 tablespoons tamari

2 teaspoons cornstarch

2 tablespoons maple syrup

¼ teaspoon garlic powder

¼ teaspoon ground ginger

Protein: 8 grams per serving (4 pieces)
Active Time: 10 minutes
Marinating Time: 1 hour
Cook Time: 40 minutes
Total Time: 1 hour 50 minutes

INSTRUCTIONS:

Puffed Tofu

1. Turn the tofu on its side and cut through the center to make two rectangles. Flip them onto their flat sides and stack. Cut through the center, and without separating the halves, cut those two halves twice each. Make two equal-size cuts lengthwise. There are now twenty-four cubes. Place the cubes in a small flat casserole dish or other container in which all the cubes will fit on one level.

2. Mix together the vegetable broth and hot sauce. Pour over the tofu. Marinate for an hour.

3. Preheat the oven to 350°F.

4. Place ¼ cup cornstarch in a medium bowl. Remove the tofu from the marinade and place on the cornstarch. Toss and then place the tofu on a baking sheet. Bake for 30 to 40 minutes. Toss with a spatula every 10 minutes until golden and puffed.

Dipping Sauce

5. To a small saucepan, add ½ cup water, tamari, and cornstarch and heat on medium high. Stir until the cornstarch is dissolved. Add the remaining ingredients and bring to a boil. Turn down heat to medium and cook, stirring until desired thickness. Place the tofu on a platter with toothpicks and dip into the sauce.

The High-Protein Vegan Cookbook

TRIPLE POWER PATTIES

YIELD: 6 SERVINGS

These patties are full of so many tasty ingredients—but there's more! There's also a spicy vegan mayo dip.

INGREDIENTS:

Patties

2 medium sweet potatoes, peeled and chopped into 2-inch cubes (equal to 2 cups mashed sweet potato)

1 cup quinoa

2 tablespoons extra virgin olive oil, divided

¼ cup diced onion

2 tablespoons raw shelled hempseed

¼ teaspoon paprika

¼ teaspoon ground cumin

¼ cup panko

1 14-ounce can black beans, drained and rinsed

Spicy Mayo Dip

½ cup vegan mayonnaise

¼ cup sweet chili sauce

1 teaspoon tamari

½ teaspoon Tabasco

INSTRUCTIONS:

Patties

1. Place the sweet potato cubes in a medium saucepan and cover with water. Cover and bring to a boil and then turn the heat down to medium high. Cook with the lid cracked a bit, about 15 minutes or until you can pierce the sweet potatoes with a fork. Drain and mash. Set aside.

2. Cook the quinoa in another saucepan: place quinoa in a sieve and rinse well. In a small saucepan, combine quinoa and ⅔ cup water. Bring to a boil, cover, and reduce to a simmer. Cook for 10 to 15 minutes or until the water is absorbed. Remove from the heat and let set with the cover on for 5 minutes. Remove lid and fluff.

3. Meanwhile, add 1 tablespoon of oil to a skillet and heat to medium high. Add the onion and sauté for about 10 to 15 minutes or until translucent.

4. To a large bowl, add the mashed potatoes, quinoa, sautéed onion, hempseed, paprika, cumin, and panko and stir well. Stir in the black beans Make twelve balls and then flatten to patties that are about ¼ inch thick.

5. Add the remaining oil to a skillet and heat to medium high. Brown the patties on each side for about 3 to 5 minutes or until lightly browned.

Spicy Mayo Dip

6. Mix all the dip ingredients together thoroughly.

7. Serve in a bowl alongside Triple Power Patties.

Protein: 6½ grams per serving (2 patties)
Active Time: 25 minutes
Cook Time: 55 minutes
Total Time: 1 hour 20 minutes

The High-Protein Vegan Cookbook

BLACK BEAN TEMPEH NACHOS WITH CASHEW CHEESE

YIELD: 4 SERVINGS

This fabulous array of ingredients is more of an assembly than a recipe. The cashew cheese is so delicious you'll want to eat it by the spoonful.

INGREDIENTS:

Cashew Cheese

¾ cup raw cashews, soaked from 1 hour to overnight and drained

1 tablespoon nutritional yeast

1 tablespoon tapioca starch or tapioca flour (they are the same thing)

½ teaspoon garlic powder

½ teaspoon onion powder

1 tablespoon lemon juice

½ cup water

Tempeh Nachos

10 to 18 ounces tortilla chips

1 15-ounce can black beans, drained and rinsed

½ cup diced red onion

1 Roma tomato, diced small

8 ounces tempeh, diced very small

1 hot chili pepper, sliced thin crosswise

2 tablespoons raw shelled hempseed

1 avocado

Juice from one lime

INSTRUCTIONS:

Cashew Cheese

1. Add all the cheese ingredients to a blender and blend until smooth. Transfer this blended mixture into a small saucepan. Cook on medium heat and stir until the sauce thickens a bit. It will take about 5 to 10 minutes. Take off the heat to cool slightly.

To Assemble the Nachos

2. Lay all the chips on a platter. Sprinkle black beans over the chips. Dot with cashew cheese. Sprinkle the red onion, tomato, tempeh, chili pepper, and hempseed all over the top.

3. Dice the avocado and dredge in lime juice. Sprinkle diced avocado over the nachos.

Protein: 27 grams per serving
Active Time: 20 minutes
Soaking Time: 1 hour
Cook Time: 10 minutes
Total Time: 1 hour 30 minutes

TOASTED PROTEIN MUSHROOM ROLLS

YIELD: 6 SERVINGS

Here's something that you probably haven't seen before. Roll some bread flat, spread with filling, roll up, and bake. Whoa!

INGREDIENTS:

¼ cup raw cashews, soaked for 1 hour

1 tablespoon plus 2 teaspoons dairy-free milk

1 teaspoon lemon juice

¼ teaspoon salt

Pinch of ground black pepper

4 ounces button mushrooms

¼ cup dairy-free butter, divided

2 tablespoons raw shelled hempseed

9 slices whole-grain bread

INSTRUCTIONS:

1. Add cashews, milk, lemon juice, salt, and pepper to a food processor. Process until smooth.

2. Clean mushrooms and finely chop.

3. Heat 1 tablespoon butter over medium-high heat in a small skillet. Add chopped mushrooms and sauté for 5 minutes. Turn off the heat and add the cashew mixture and hempseed. Stir well.

4. Preheat the oven to 425°F.

5. Cut crusts off of the bread and leave in a square shape. Roll each square thin with a rolling pin. You will be rolling up these squares. Spread 1 tablespoon mushroom mixture onto each square and roll up.

6. Melt remaining butter.

7. Cut rolls in half and roll in melted butter. Place rolls on cookie sheets and bake for 8 minutes or until browned.

Protein: 18 grams per serving (3 rolls)
Active Time: 20 minutes
Soaking Time: 1 hour
Cook Time: 15 minutes
Total Time: 1 hour 35 minutes

ARTICHOKE QUINOA DIP

This is a nice versatile dip. It also can be used as a spread on mini toasts or stuffed into a variety of vegetables, such as mini bell peppers. All are good appetizers in their own right.

INGREDIENTS:

- ½ cup quinoa
- 1 tablespoon extra virgin olive oil
- ½ cup diced onion
- 4 ounces baby spinach, with stems chopped off
- ¼ cup raw shelled hempseed
- ½ teaspoon onion powder
- ½ teaspoon garlic powder
- 1 teaspoon salt
- ¼ teaspoon ground black pepper
- 8 ounces artichoke hearts in water, drained
- 1 tablespoon lemon juice

INSTRUCTIONS:

1. Place quinoa in a sieve and rinse well. Combine quinoa and 1 cup water in a small saucepan. Bring to a boil, cover, and reduce to a simmer. Cook for 10 to 15 minutes or until the liquid is absorbed. Remove from the heat and let set with the cover on for 5 minutes. Remove lid and fluff.

2. Heat the oil in a large skillet over medium-high heat. Add the onion and sauté over medium heat for 10 minutes. Stir in the spinach and cook until wilted, about a minute or so. Add the hempseed and spices and stir in quickly. Remove from the heat.

3. Cut off the top of the artichoke hearts. Discard the toughest of the outside leaves.

4. Add everything to a food processor. Process until well combined and chopped very small.

5. Serve with homemade pita chips (see note).

Note: Making homemade pita chips is a very simple process: Buy a bag of pita pockets or flatbread. Brush pita pockets with oil and cut into triangles. Lay on a baking sheet. Bake at 400°F for about 5 to 7 minutes. Watch very closely to make sure they do not burn.

Protein: 10 grams per serving
Active Time: 20 minutes
Cook Time: 25 minutes
Total Time: 45 minutes

BAKED SEITAN SWIRLS

YIELD: 6 SERVINGS

These soft, sturdy bites are perfect for dipping. They're satisfying, with spicy seitan rolled inside. Serve these swirls with sauces of your choice. You control the heat.

INGREDIENTS:

½ cup all-purpose flour

½ cup whole wheat flour

1 tablespoon coconut sugar

1 teaspoon baking powder

½ teaspoon baking soda

¼ teaspoon salt

5 tablespoons coconut oil, melted

6 tablespoons dairy-free milk

8 ounces seitan (Slow Cooker Log for Thin Slices and Crumbles, page 280)

Mustards, for serving

INSTRUCTIONS:

1. Preheat the oven to 350°F.

2. Add the flours, sugar, baking powder, baking soda, and salt to a medium bowl. Mix well.

3. In a small bowl, combine the oil and milk. Stir into the dry mixture to make a stiff dough.

4. Roll the dough out into about an 8-inch square. Cut lengthwise down the center so that there are two rectangles measuring 4 by 8 inches.

5. Put the seitan in a food processor and process for crumbles. Divide the seitan in half and spread across each dough rectangle leaving 1 inch on the long side of each rectangle. Start rolling up, lengthwise, and end at the edge that has no seitan. Roll firmly but not tightly. Leave seam side. Cut each roll into ¾-inch rounds. You will end up with twelve rounds for each roll. Place about 1½ inches apart on a baking sheet and bake for 15 minutes.

6. Serve with assorted mustards.

Protein: 16 grams per serving (4 swirls)
Active Time: 15 minutes
Cook Time: 15 minutes
Total Time: 30 minutes

The High-Protein Vegan Cookbook

TEMPEH STUFFED CREMINI MUSHROOMS

YIELD: 6 SERVINGS

Here's a twist on stuffed mushrooms. There's no bread or panko in the filling, just lots of flavor along with rice and tempeh.

INGREDIENTS:

18 cremini mushrooms

2 tablespoons diced red onion, small dice

3 ounces tempeh, diced very small, or pulsed small

Pinch of onion powder

Pinch of cayenne pepper

¼ cup rice, cooked

1 tablespoon tamari

INSTRUCTIONS:

1. Remove stems from the mushrooms and set the caps aside. Finely chop the stems and set aside.

2. Heat 3 tablespoons of water in a medium skillet. Add the chopped mushroom stems and onion. Sauté 10 to 15 minutes or until onion is translucent. Add the tempeh and cook another 5 minutes. Add onion powder, cayenne pepper, rice, and tamari. Cook 2 minutes, stirring occasionally.

3. Preheat the oven to 350°F.

4. Stuff mushroom caps and place on baking sheet. Bake for 20 minutes.

Protein: 6 grams per serving (3 mushrooms)
Active Time: 15 minutes
Cook Time: 20 minutes
Total Time: 35 minutes

ROASTED TACO-SEASONED EDAMAME AND CHICKPEAS

YIELD: 7 SERVINGS

Get out a little container and fill it up with these easy-to-carry spicy protein nibbles. Baked to just the right crispness, they are made to enjoy on your day out.

INGREDIENTS:

12 ounces frozen edamame

1 15-ounce can chickpeas, drained (save the liquid to use as aquafaba) and rinsed

4 tablespoons taco seasoning

3 tablespoons aquafaba

INSTRUCTIONS:

1. Preheat the oven to 400°F.

2. Cook the edamame according to directions on package.

3. Spread the chickpeas and cooked edamame on a baking sheet. Bake for 20 minutes.

4. Place the taco seasoning in a medium bowl.

5. Remove the edamame and chickpeas from oven and toss with the aquafaba. Add to the bowl of taco seasoning and coat well.

6. Return to oven and bake another 10 minutes.

7. You can eat these as soon as they've cooled enough to handle, but let them cool in the oven for at least 2 hours to overnight before packing away. Store in an airtight container. They will keep for 2 weeks.

Protein: 7½ grams per serving (½ cup)
Active Time: 10 minutes
Cook Time: 40 minutes
Total Time: 50 minutes

SLOW COOKER SPICED PEANUTS

YIELD: 6 SERVINGS

These slow cooker peanuts are delicious and easy to make. People will think you paid a lot of money for them, and that they must have come in a beautiful tin.

INGREDIENTS:

3   cups peanuts

2   teaspoons extra virgin olive oil

½   teaspoon ground cumin

½   teaspoon powdered garlic

½   teaspoon cayenne powder

½   teaspoon smoked paprika

½   teaspoon salt

INSTRUCTIONS:

Put the peanuts in a slow cooker. Add the oil and stir so that there is a little bit of oil on all the peanuts. It will be enough. Add the spices and stir. Cook on low for 1 hour. Uncover and then cook 15 more minutes.

Protein: 19 grams per serving (½ cup)
Active Time: 10 minutes
Cook Time: 1 hour 15 minutes
Total Time: 1 hour 25 minutes

MAPLE-GLAZED MIXED NUTS

YIELD: 6 SERVINGS

This easy-to-make protein snack only takes minutes. The result is maple-sweet candied nuts that would be a gift of love for anyone.

INGREDIENTS:

1   cup walnuts

1   cup pecans

1   cup cashews

1½ cups maple syrup

INSTRUCTIONS:

1. Preheat the oven to 325°F.

2. Mix the nuts and maple syrup together in a medium bowl. Make sure that each nut has been coated well. Spread out on a baking sheet so they are in one layer but still close to each other. Touching is okay. Bake for 7 minutes.

3. Remove from oven and flip with a spatula. They can overlap some at this point. Put back in the oven and bake another 6 minutes or so. Watch closely. If they're in too long, they start to burn quickly.

4. Take the baking sheet out of the oven, flip the nuts again, and let cool completely. Eat right away or pack in an airtight container. These nuts will keep in your pantry for quite a few weeks and will keep in the fridge about 2 to 3 months. The freezer will store them for 6 months.

Protein: 10 grams per serving (½ cup)
Active Time: 5 minutes
Cook Time: 15 minutes
Total Time: 20 minutes

The High-Protein Vegan Cookbook

CHAPTER TWO

BREAKFAST POWER

SEITAN MAPLE LINKS BREAKFAST SANDWICH

YIELD: 2 SERVINGS

Tender seitan links from the slow cooker are the star of this hearty and flavorful breakfast.

INGREDIENTS:

1   tablespoon extra virgin olive oil

8   ounces mushrooms, sliced

1   tablespoon dairy-free butter

1   cup Slow Cooker Maple Breakfast Links (page 276)

2   English muffins, sliced

Condiments of choice

½   avocado, sliced

INSTRUCTIONS:

1. Heat the oil over medium-high heat in a large skillet. Add the mushrooms and sauté for about 15 minutes. Remove mushrooms from the pan and set aside.

2. Add the butter to the pan at medium-high heat. Add the links to the pan and brown on all sides for about 5 minutes total. If you made the larger size of links, then slice lengthwise through the center and fry that way. The links are already cooked all the way through and they can be enjoyed cold, but this finishes off the sandwich nicely.

3. While the links are browning, toast the English muffins and spread with your favorite condiments, such as dairy-free chipotle mayo. Layer on the sautéed mushrooms, links, and avocado. Top with English muffin slice.

Protein: 34 grams per serving
Active Time: 15 minutes
Cook Time: 20 minutes
Total Time: 35 minutes

VANILLA BREAKFAST SMOOTHIE

YIELD: 1 SERVING

This smoothie is perfect for an eclectic plant-based breakfast. You need only seven ingredients, and you can make it in less than 10 minutes.

INGREDIENTS:

1   frozen banana, sliced

1   cup vanilla almond milk

¼   cup old-fashioned oats

¼   cup raisins

1   tablespoon flaxseed meal

¼   teaspoon cinnamon

3   tablespoons vanilla protein powder

INSTRUCTIONS:

Add all the ingredients to a blender and blend until very smooth.

Protein: 20 grams per serving
Active Time: 10 minutes
Total Time: 10 minutes

TO THE POWER OF FOUR OVERNIGHT OATS

YIELD: 2 SERVINGS

If you haven't had overnight oats before, then here is a fantastic recipe that will make you a believer. It's simple to the nth degree and features everyone's favorite ingredients.

INGREDIENTS:

3½ cups unsweetened almond milk

2 cups old-fashioned oats

¼ cup maple syrup

2 tablespoons chia seeds

2 tablespoons unsweetened shredded coconut

¼ cup sunflower seed kernels

4 tablespoons peanut butter, divided

Sunflower seed kernels, for garnish (optional)

INSTRUCTIONS:

1. Add all the ingredients except for 2 tablespoons of the peanut butter and the sunflower seeds to a large bowl. Mix well. It will seem very wet but the chia seeds and oats will absorb some of the milk. Cover and place in the refrigerator to set overnight.

2. To serve in the morning, dot the remaining 2 tablespoons peanut butter around the inside of two bowls and fill each with the overnight oats. Garnish with sunflower seeds, if desired.

Protein: 23 grams per serving
Active Time: 10 minutes
Overnight Time: 8 hours
Total Time: 8 hours 10 minutes

WARM MAPLE PROTEIN OATMEAL

YIELD: 2 SERVINGS

Do you keep forgetting about oatmeal? If you make this recipe, you'll never forget again. Healthy, warm, and mildly sweet, this oatmeal dish will have you humming through breakfast.

INGREDIENTS:

1   cup steel-cut oats

3   tablespoons raw shelled hempseed, divided

3   tablespoons maple syrup

2   teaspoons cinnamon

1   tablespoon slivered almonds

1   tablespoon currants

INSTRUCTIONS:

1. Bring 4 cups of water to a boil in a large sauce-pan. Add the steel-cut oatmeal, 2 tablespoons hempseed, maple syrup, and cinnamon and bring back to a boil. Reduce heat to low and cook uncovered for 30 minutes, stirring occasionally.

2. Serve in bowls, garnished with almond slivers, currants, and the remaining hempseed.

Protein: 23 grams per serving
Active Time: 5 minutes
Cook Time: 30 minutes
Total Time: 35 minutes

SAVORY QUINOA BREAKFAST CUPS

YIELD: 6 SERVINGS

Muffins are always a nice grab-and-go breakfast. Neat and filling. Another nice thing about them is that you can enjoy them at your leisure.

INGREDIENTS:

½ cup plus 3 tablespoons quinoa

½ cup spinach

½ cup sliced mushrooms

1 cup milk

⅓ cup chickpea flour

1 tablespoon nutritional yeast

2 tablespoons raw shelled hempseed

½ teaspoon salt

INSTRUCTIONS:

1. Place the quinoa in a sieve and rinse well. In a small saucepan, combine quinoa and 1 cup plus 2 tablespoons water. Bring to a boil, cover, and reduce to a simmer. Cook for 10 to 15 minutes or until the liquid is absorbed. Remove from the heat and let set with the cover on for 5 minutes. Remove the lid and fluff.

2. Preheat the oven to 375°F.

3. Place paper muffin cups in a six-cup muffin tin.

4. Place spinach and mushrooms in a food processor and process until finely chopped.

5. Add all the ingredients to a large bowl and mix well.

6. Divide the mixture between muffin cups. Bake for 20 to 25 minutes.

Protein: 7 grams per serving
Active Time: 10 minutes
Cook Time: 40 minutes
Total Time: 50 minutes

The High-Protein Vegan Cookbook

HIGH-PROTEIN CHOCOLATE BLENDER MUFFINS

YIELD: 6 SERVINGS

These moist and chocolaty muffins will leave you feeling guilt-free. Blend, pour, and bake for an easy road to chocolate protein.

INGREDIENTS:

1   15-ounce can black beans, drained and rinsed

½   cup applesauce

2   tablespoons ground chia seeds

¼   cup dairy-free milk

1   tablespoon lemon juice

½   cup maple syrup

2   teaspoons vanilla extract

1   tablespoon flaxseed

½   cup unsweetened cocoa powder

1   teaspoon baking powder

½   teaspoon baking soda

½   cup old-fashioned oats

½   cup dairy-free chocolate chips

¼   cup raw shelled hempseed

INSTRUCTIONS:

1. Preheat the oven to 350°F.

2. Line a twelve-cup muffin tin with paper liners.

3. Place all the ingredients in a blender except the chocolate chips and the hempseed. Blend until the mixture is as smooth as possible. Add the chocolate chips and hempseed and blend 5 seconds or until dispersed.

4. Pour into the muffin cups, filling at least three-quarters full. Bake for 20 minutes. Cool for 5 minutes, and then move the paper cups to a wire rack to cool completely.

5. Store in the refrigerator for up to 3 days or freeze up to 6 months.

Protein: 14 grams per serving (2 muffins)
Active Time: 15 minutes
Cook Time: 20 minutes
Total Time: 35 minutes

LEMON STRAWBERRY PROTEIN MUFFINS

YIELD: 6 SERVINGS

All you need is one of these big fat muffins to make you feel full and satisfied. Strawberries are added for that contrasting fruity touch that we all crave now and again.

INGREDIENTS:

2   tablespoons ground chia seeds or chia seeds, divided

5   tablespoons dairy-free butter

½   cup coconut sugar

½   cup plus 2 tablespoons dairy-free milk

1   tablespoon lemon juice

1½ cups whole wheat flour

1½ teaspoons baking powder

½   teaspoon baking soda

¼   teaspoon salt

¼   cup raw shelled hempseed

½   cup strawberries, chopped

INSTRUCTIONS:

1. Preheat the oven to 375°F.

2. Grease the inside of a six-cup muffin tin and set aside.

3. Mix 1 tablespoon ground chia seeds together with 3 tablespoons water and set aside.

4. Using an electric mixer, beat together the butter and sugar in a large bowl until light and fluffy, about 3 minutes. Add the chia seed mixture and mix again. Add the milk and lemon juice. Mix well.

5. Add the flour, baking powder, baking soda, salt, hempseed, and the remaining tablespoon ground chia seeds to a medium bowl. Mix. Add the flour mixture to the wet mixture and beat until just combined. It will be a sticky batter. Fold in the strawberries.

6. Divide the batter between the muffin cups. Fill at least three-quarters full, even if you're short on filling for one cup. Bake for 25 minutes or until a toothpick inserted into the center comes out clean.

Protein: 10 grams per serving (1 muffin)
Active Time: 15 minutes
Cook Time: 25 minutes
Total Time: 40 minutes

CRAZY QUINOA PROTEIN MUFFINS

YIELD: 6 SERVINGS

These cute little muffins are crispy on the outside and cake-like on the inside. Sweetened with raisins and maple syrup, they will tempt you whenever they're around.

INGREDIENTS:

- ½ cup quinoa
- 2 tablespoons ground chia seeds or chia seeds
- ¼ cup almond flour
- 3 tablespoons vanilla protein powder
- ½ teaspoon salt
- ½ cup dates, chopped small
- 2 tablespoons coconut oil
- 3 tablespoons maple syrup
- 1 teaspoon vanilla extract
- ¼ cup unsweetened shredded coconut
- ½ cup raisins

INSTRUCTIONS:

1. Rinse the quinoa and place in a small saucepan with a lid. Cover with ½ cup water and bring to a boil over medium-high heat. Cover and turn down to low. Let cook for 20 minutes and then remove from the heat. Take off the lid and let cool.

2. Preheat the oven to 450°F. Line six muffin cups with paper liners.

3. Mix the ground chia seeds with ¼ cup plus 2 tablespoons water and set aside.

4. Add the almond flour, protein powder, and salt to a small bowl. Mix well. Add the dates and mix to coat. Set aside.

5. Put the coconut oil in a medium bowl. If it is not liquid already, put in the microwave and heat for 10 to 20 seconds or until melted. Remove from microwave and add the maple syrup. Stir well. When cool, add the chia seed mixture, vanilla extract, coconut, almond flour mixture, cooked quinoa, and raisins. Mix well.

6. Divide the batter between the six muffin cups and bake 12 to 15 minutes, until a toothpick inserted in the center comes out clean.

Protein: 7 grams per serving (1 muffin)
Active Time: 15 minutes
Cook Time: 35 minutes
Total Time: 50 minutes

MULTI-LAYERED AVOCADO TOAST

YIELD: 2 SERVINGS

Avocado toast meets the breakfast brunch. Toast topped with protein, fiber, and taste makes for a simple breakfast that's good enough for a midmorning snack, too.

INGREDIENTS:

1 tablespoon dairy-free butter

4 ounces extra-firm tofu, drained and pressed (page 17)

¼ teaspoon black salt

¼ teaspoon onion powder

Pinch of turmeric

1 avocado

Pinch of ground black pepper

1 teaspoon lime juice

2 slices sprouted grain bread

INSTRUCTIONS:

1. Add the butter to a skillet and heat over medium-high heat. Crumble tofu into the skillet. Sprinkle with the salt, onion powder, and turmeric and sauté for about 4 minutes, making sure the tofu is crumbled small.

2. In a small bowl, mash the avocado with the pepper and lime juice.

3. Toast the bread. Spread half of the prepared avocado on each piece of toast. Top with half of the prepared tofu on each piece of toast. Slice the toasts in half at an angle.

Protein: 16 grams per serving
Active Time: 15 minutes
Cook Time: 5 minutes
Total Time: 20 minutes

SOUTHWEST SCRAMBLE BREAKFAST BURRITO

YIELD: 2 SERVINGS

This recipe is one step beyond scrambled tofu. Take a little extra time to add the veggies and spices, then roll it all up snugly in a tortilla. The result is both filling and special.

INGREDIENTS:

- 1 tablespoon dairy-free butter
- ½ cup diced red bell pepper
- ½ cup diced red onion
- 8 ounces extra-firm tofu, drained and pressed (page 17)
- ½ cup Steamed Seitan Chipotle Links, crumbled (page 284)
- 1 tablespoon taco seasoning
- ½ teaspoon salt
- 2 tablespoons flaxseed meal
- 2 large sprouted grain tortillas

INSTRUCTIONS:

1. Melt the butter in a large skillet over medium-high heat. Add the bell pepper and onion and sauté for 10 minutes. Crumble in the tofu along with the prepared seitan. Sauté for 5 minutes more and add the taco seasoning and salt. Sprinkle in flaxseed meal and mix well.

2. Spoon half the mixture into each tortilla and roll burrito-style. Cut in half and serve.

Protein: 41 grams per serving
Active Time: 10 minutes
Cook Time: 15 minutes
Total Time: 25 minutes

CHOCOLATE BANANA HEMP SMOOTHIE BOWL

YIELD: 1 SERVING

There's nothing like hiding a bit of spinach in a chocolate banana smoothie bowl. Make it for breakfast and you're off to a running start for the day.

INGREDIENTS:

Smoothie Bowl

1 frozen banana, 4 slices reserved for topping

½ cup almond milk or other dairy-free milk

1 tablespoon almond butter

1 tablespoon cocoa powder

1 tablespoon maple syrup

1 cup spinach

Toppings

4 banana slices (from above)

1 strawberry, sliced

2 tablespoons dairy-free chocolate chips

2 tablespoons raw shelled hempseed

INSTRUCTIONS:

1. Add the smoothie bowl ingredients to a blender and blend until smooth.

2. Pour into a bowl and garnish with the toppings.

Protein: 23 grams per serving
Active Time: 10 minutes
Total Time: 10 minutes

SEEDS, NUTS, AND FRUIT BAKED GRANOLA

YIELD: 8 SERVINGS

This recipe makes an abundant amount, which will keep for about a month. A protein-packed cereal in the morning is a terrific way to start a day, especially when it's as simple as pouring it into a bowl. You can add even more protein with a plant-based milk.

INGREDIENTS:

7   cups old-fashioned oats (use gluten-free if desired)

1   cup shredded coconut

1   cup sunflower seed kernels

1   cup walnuts

1   cup coconut sugar

¼   cup chia seeds

1   cup coconut oil

1   cup raisins

INSTRUCTIONS:

1. Preheat the oven to 300°F.

2. Mix all the ingredients together except for the raisins. Spread out in a large baking pan.

3. Bake for 40 minutes. Take out of the oven every 10 minutes and stir. Return to the oven.

4. After 30 minutes, add raisins and stir. Bake for 10 more minutes. Take out of the oven and let cool.

5. Pack in airtight container. Will keep for 4 weeks.

Protein: 16 grams per serving
Active Time: 10 minutes
Cook Time: 40 minutes
Total Time: 50 minutes

BLUEBERRY TOFU PANCAKES

YIELD: 4 SERVINGS

There's nothing wrong with treating yourself to a little bit of something sweet in the morning, especially when it's going over pancakes packed with tofu and oats.

INGREDIENTS:

2 tablespoons flaxseed meal

8 ounces extra-firm tofu, drained and pressed (page 17)

½ cup old-fashioned oats

1¼ cups dairy-free milk

1 cup all-purpose flour

3 tablespoons coconut sugar

1 teaspoon vanilla extract

1 teaspoon baking powder

1 teaspoon ground cinnamon

½ teaspoon salt

½ teaspoon plus 1 tablespoon extra virgin olive oil, divided

¼ cup maple syrup, for serving

½ cup frozen blueberries, defrosted, divided

INSTRUCTIONS:

1. Mix the flaxseed meal with 6 tablespoons water and set aside.

2. Add all the ingredients except the blueberries and 1 tablespoon oil to a food processor and blend well. Use the quick pulse button to blend in ¼ cup of the blueberries.

3. Heat the remaining oil in a skillet and add ¼ cup of the pancake batter to the center of the pan. When bubbling on one side, flip and cook until golden brown. Continue until all the batter is gone.

4. Serve with maple syrup and remaining ¼ cup blueberries sprinkled on top.

Protein: 17 grams per serving (3 pancakes)
Active Time: 10 minutes
Cook Time: 10 minutes
Total Time: 20 minutes

CHOCOLATE STRAWBERRY CHIA SEED PUDDING

YIELD: 2 SERVINGS

Get your fruit *and* protein in this breakfast treat. Make this pudding recipe the night before for a simple fruit-filled breakfast that only takes a few minutes of prep time.

INGREDIENTS:

1   cup dairy-free milk

⅓   cup dates

½   cup strawberries (more for garnish, optional)

2   tablespoons cocoa powder

½   teaspoon vanilla extract

¼   cup ground chia seeds

3   tablespoons raw shelled hempseed

2   tablespoons maple syrup

Shaved chocolate, for garnish (optional)

INSTRUCTIONS:

1. Add the milk and dates to a blender. Blend until smooth. Add the strawberries, cocoa powder, vanilla, ground chia seeds, hempseed, and maple syrup. Blend well. Pour into two bowls and refrigerate for at least 4 hours.

2. Garnish with shaved chocolate and pieces of strawberry, if desired.

Protein: 16 grams per serving
Active Time: 15 minutes
Chill Time: 4 hours
Total Time: 4 hours 15 minutes

SPROUTED GRAIN TOAST WITH NUT BUTTER AND BANANA

YIELD: 2 SERVINGS

This is more of a how-to than a recipe, but believe me, if it isn't written down in a cookbook you might forget about it. And you don't want to forget about it. How can something so simple taste so good?

INGREDIENTS:

2   slices sprouted grain bread

¼   cup peanut butter

¼   cup raw shelled hempseed

1   banana, sliced

INSTRUCTIONS:

Toast bread. Cut in half at an angle. Spread 2 tablespoons peanut butter on each slice of toast. Sprinkle the hempseed on each triangle of toast and layer slices of banana on top.

Protein: 11 grams per serving
Active Time: 10 minutes
Total Time: 10 minutes

PEANUT BUTTER BANANA BREAKFAST COOKIES

YIELD: 24 SERVINGS

You won't believe the list of ingredients that make up these healthful protein cookies. They are rustic in looks and satisfying in quality.

INGREDIENTS:

2   bananas, mashed

⅓   cup creamy peanut butter

⅔   cup unsweetened applesauce

¼   cup almond flour

2   tablespoons raw shelled hempseed

1   teaspoon vanilla extract

1½ cups quick-cooking oats

½   cup pitted dates, chopped

INSTRUCTIONS:

1. Preheat the oven to 350°F.

2. Line a baking sheet with parchment paper and set aside.

3. Add the mashed banana and peanut butter to a large bowl and mix well. Add the applesauce, flour, hempseed, and vanilla. Mix well. Stir in the oatmeal and dates.

4. Drop cookie dough, 1 heaping tablespoon at a time and 2 inches apart, onto the prepared baking sheet. Flatten with the back of a fork. Bake cookies for 25 minutes.

5. Remove from the oven and let the cookies cool 5 minutes, then move to a cooling rack.

Protein: 7¾ grams per serving (3 cookies)
Active Time: 10 minutes
Cook Time: 25 minutes
Total Time: 35 minutes

Note: You can also freeze these cookies after baking. Pack in a freezer bag and store in the freezer for up to 6 months. Remove as many cookies as you like for breakfast. They will take about 30 minutes to defrost at room temperature.

SEITAN LINKS TOFU SCRAMBLE

YIELD: 6 SERVINGS

A scramble is one of the easiest ways to prepare tofu. Take it a step further and add some veggies and seitan and you've got a major power breakfast.

INGREDIENTS:

1 tablespoon dairy-free butter

½ cup diced onion

8 ounces mushrooms, sliced

16 ounces extra-firm tofu, drained, pressed (page 17), and crumbled

8 ounces Slow Cooker Maple Breakfast Links, sliced thick (page 276)

1 15-ounce can black beans, drained and rinsed

2 tablespoons nutritional yeast

½ teaspoon chili powder

½ teaspoon paprika

½ teaspoon black salt

½ teaspoon turmeric

¼ teaspoon garlic powder

INSTRUCTIONS:

1. Heat the butter over medium-high heat in a large skillet. Add the onion, mushrooms, tofu, and seitan links. Sauté 15 minutes.

2. Add the black beans, nutritional yeast, and all the spices and seasonings. Heat through 5 minutes and serve.

Protein: 29 grams per serving
Active Time: 15 minutes
Cook Time: 20 minutes
Total Time: 35 minutes

BUCKWHEAT COCONUT PORRIDGE

YIELD: 2 SERVINGS

Here's your chance to use buckwheat! Buckwheat becomes porridge in this recipe. It's a delicious breakfast that will keep you fueled for a long time.

INGREDIENTS:

1   cup creamy buckwheat cereal

½   teaspoon ground cinnamon

¼   teaspoon salt

¼   cup peanut butter

½   cup coconut cream

¼   cup cranberries

¼   cup pecans

2   tablespoons raw shelled hempseed

¼   cup maple syrup

INSTRUCTIONS:

1. Bring 3 cups of water to a boil in a medium saucepan. Add the cereal, cinnamon, and salt. Reduce the heat to medium low and cover. Cook for 8 minutes, stirring occasionally, until all the water is absorbed. Stir in peanut butter and coconut cream.

2. Serve in two bowls and garnish with the cranberries, pecans, hempseed, and maple syrup.

Protein: 20 grams per serving
Active Time: 15 minutes
Cook Time: 10 minutes
Total Time: 25 minutes

SLOW COOKER APPLES AND OATS

YIELD: 2 SERVINGS

Here's a wonderful breakfast you'll want over and over again. This dish serves two or three people, but it can easily be doubled or tripled for a larger family.

INGREDIENTS:

1½ cups peeled and sliced apples (I like them kind of thick)

1 cup old-fashioned oats

½ cup dairy-free butter, melted

½ cup coconut sugar

2 tablespoons lemon juice

2 tablespoons hempseed, toasted in shell

1 teaspoon ground cinnamon

1 cup pecans, chopped

INSTRUCTIONS:

Put all the ingredients in the slow cooker and stir. Turn to high (it must cook on high). Cook 2 to 3 hours, depending on your preference of doneness. Serve hot, warm, or cool.

Protein: 15 grams per serving
Active Time: 15 minutes
Cook Time: 3 hours
Total Time: 3 hours 15 minutes

The High-Protein Vegan Cookbook

OVERNIGHT MUESLI

YIELD: 6 SERVINGS

Overnight breakfasts aren't only for oats. Making this homemade muesli recipe is as easy as measuring ingredients into a bowl. As an extra bonus, it keeps for days.

INGREDIENTS:

2   cups old-fashioned oats

1   cup raisins

½   cup wheat germ

½   cup oat bran

½   cup dates, chopped

½   cup pepitas

¼   cup wheat bran

¼   cup slivered almonds

¼   cup walnuts, chopped

¼   cup sunflower seed kernels

7   cups almond milk or other dairy-free milk

INSTRUCTIONS:

1. Place all the dry ingredients in a large mixing bowl. Mix well. Pour in the milk and mix well again.

2. Cover and place in the refrigerator to sit overnight.

3. The muesli is ready to eat in the morning and keeps for 4 to 5 days.

Protein: 15 grams per serving
Active Time: 15 minutes
Total Time: 15 minutes and then overnight

ALL-IN-ONE SKILLET BREAKFAST HASH

YIELD: 6 SERVINGS

Here's a hardy breakfast that will feed a large group with satisfaction guaranteed. This will stick to your ribs, just as any good protein meal should.

INGREDIENTS:

2   tablespoons coconut oil

2   cups diced russet potatoes

2   cups diced sweet potatoes

1   cup diced white onion

8   ounces extra-firm tofu, drained and pressed (page 17)

2   teaspoons black salt

1½ teaspoons onion powder

1½ teaspoons garlic powder

½   teaspoon turmeric

½   teaspoon thyme

¼   teaspoon ground black pepper

2   cups Slow Cooker Maple Breakfast Links, sliced (page 276)

2   tablespoons nutritional yeast

INSTRUCTIONS:

1. In a very large skillet, either 12 inches wide or very deep, heat the oil over medium-high heat. Add the russet potatoes and cook for 10 minutes, flipping once. Add the sweet potatoes and onion; stir and cook 5 more minutes.

2. Push the potatoes and onions to the side and crumble the tofu into the pan. Add all of the spices and mix with the tofu. Cook 2 to 3 minutes or until you see that the turmeric is dispersed well and the tofu has turned a golden color.

3. Add the links and nutritional yeast and mix the whole skillet of ingredients together. Cook 2 to 3 minutes or until the links are heated through. Taste and season with more salt and pepper, if desired.

Protein: 30 grams per serving
Active Time: 15 minutes
Cook Time: 25 minutes
Total Time: 40 minutes

The High-Protein Vegan Cookbook

MIXED PROTEIN ENCHILADA BREAKFAST

YIELD: 6 SERVINGS

These cheesy enchiladas are filling enough for a huge day on the weekend and complex enough for a very satisfying breakfast or dinner. The tofu and seitan are both stars.

INGREDIENTS:

Filling

1¼ cups Steamed Seitan Chipotle Links (page 284)

1½ cups broccoli florets

1 tablespoon coconut oil

4 ounces extra-firm tofu, drained and pressed (page 17)

1 tablespoon nutritional yeast

1½ teaspoons black salt

¾ teaspoon ground black pepper, divided

¼ teaspoon turmeric

¼ teaspoon paprika

1 15-ounce can pinto beans, drained and rinsed

1 teaspoon salt

White Cheese Sauce

2 tablespoons dairy-free butter

3 tablespoons flour

1½ cups dairy-free milk

2 tablespoons nutritional yeast

½ teaspoon salt

Protein: 28 grams per serving
Active Time: 40 minutes
Cook Time: 40 minutes
Total Time: 1 hour 20 minutes

To Assemble:

1 15-ounce can enchilada sauce

6 flour tortillas, 8 to 10 inches in diameter

Black olives, sliced, for garnish

Green onions, sliced, for garnish

Cilantro, chopped, for garnish

INSTRUCTIONS:

Filling

1. Place the seitan pieces in a food processor and pulse until lightly crumbled.

2. Add water to a medium saucepan with a steamer insert and bring to a boil. Add the broccoli to the insert and steam over boiling water for 10 minutes. Remove from steamer and set aside.

3. Heat the oil in a large skillet over medium-high heat. Crumble the tofu into the skillet, using your hands. Stir and cook for 3 minutes, breaking up any pieces that are still too large. Add the nutritional yeast, black salt, ½ teaspoon pepper, turmeric, and paprika. Stir to combine. Add the seitan, beans, broccoli, salt, and ¼ teaspoon pepper. Stir to combine. Remove from the heat and set aside.

White Cheese Sauce

4. Melt the butter in a medium saucepan over medium-high heat. Add the flour and stir, cooking for 1 minute. Add the milk and bring to a low boil. Stir occasionally to keep the lumps out of the sauce. Turn the heat down to medium and add nutritional yeast and salt. Stir and continue to cook to let thicken a bit. Remove from the heat and set aside.

Assembly

5. Preheat the oven to 350°F.

6. In a 9-inch square or 8-by-10-inch casserole dish, add 3 tablespoons of the enchilada sauce. Spread over the bottom.

7. Divide the filling in the skillet into six portions. You can eyeball this or make creases in the filling in a pie shape.

8. Lay out a tortilla and lightly spread with enchilada sauce. Fill with a sixth of the tofu filling. Roll up and place in the casserole dish. Continue until all six tortillas have been filled and rolled. Pour the remaining enchilada sauce over the top of the rolled tortillas.

9. Heat the white cheese sauce again if it has thickened, so that you can spoon it over the top of the enchilada sauce. Cover and bake for 30 minutes.

10. Uncover, garnish with olives, green onions, and cilantro, and serve.

CHAPTER THREE

LUNCH BOWLS, CHILIES, AND SANDWICHES

APPLE BROCCOLI CRUNCH BOWL

YIELD: 6 SERVINGS

Here's a bowl that's filled with everyone's favorite vegetables and fruits. Simply throw all the ingredients into a bowl and then pour on the slightly sweet and tangy dressing. Toss and eat!

INGREDIENTS:

Bowl

2   medium heads broccoli (about 4 cups when chopped)

3   apples of your choice, diced right before you add them to the salad (I use Gala)

¼   cup diced red onion

½   cup raisins

½   cup sunflower seed kernels

¼   cup raw shelled hempseed

Dressing

¼   cup cider vinegar

½   cup extra virgin olive oil

2   cloves garlic, minced

1   tablespoon maple syrup (you can use up to 2 tablespoons)

½   teaspoon salt

¼   teaspoon ground black pepper

INSTRUCTIONS:

Bowl

1. Cut the florets from the broccoli stalks and set the stalks aside. Cut the florets into very small pieces. Place in a large bowl.

2. Cut the hard outer skin off the broccoli stalks to get down to the tender inside. Discard the outer skin. Cut the inside stems into matchsticks. (Or you can use a mandolin or food processor that has an attachment that will cut the stems into long strips—not grated. Scissors work too.) The idea is to have very small sticks of raw broccoli stems that will hold their shape. Add to the large bowl along with the florets. Add the apples, onions, raisins, sunflower seeds, and hempseed.

Dressing

3. Whisk together all of the dressing ingredients in a medium bowl. Add the dressing to the salad and toss. Chill until ready to serve.

Protein: 9 grams per serving
Active Time: 20 minutes
Total Time: 20 minutes

SMOKY TEMPEH BUDDHA BOWL

YIELD: 2 SERVINGS

A warm and colorful lunch is something worth your time. The ingredients in this bowl act as complements to each other, with the added bonus of protein.

INGREDIENTS:

Bowl

1   small sweet potato, chopped into bite-size pieces

1   tablespoon extra virgin olive oil

½   teaspoon salt

¼   cup dry quinoa

½   cup vegetable broth

4   ounces faux bacon-flavored tempeh

Almond Curry Sauce

3   tablespoons almond butter

3   tablespoons dairy-free milk

1½ tablespoons tamari

1   tablespoon rice vinegar

1   tablespoon red curry paste

To Assemble

2½ cups baby spinach

½   cup chopped red bell pepper

½   cup chopped purple cabbage

INSTRUCTIONS:

Bowl

1. Preheat the oven to 375°F.

2. Place the sweet potatoes on a baking sheet. Drizzle the oil over the top and lightly toss. Sprinkle with salt. Bake for 30 to 35 minutes or until they can be easily pierced with a fork. Set aside.

3. Meanwhile, cook the quinoa. Place quinoa in a sieve and rinse well. In a small saucepan, combine quinoa and broth. Bring to a boil, cover, and reduce to a simmer. Cook for 10 to 15 minutes or until the broth is absorbed. Remove from the heat and let set with the cover on for 5 minutes.

4. Cut the tempeh into ¼-inch slices and then cube.

Almond Curry Sauce

5. Mix all the ingredients together in a small bowl until smooth and well combined.

Assembly

6. Fill each salad bowl with the spinach. Make a decorative rim with the spinach tips if so desired. Divide the quinoa and vegetables between the two bowls and lay in a circle: peppers, quinoa, cabbage, sweet potatoes, and lastly, tempeh. Drizzle the dressing in a circle over all.

Protein: 15 grams per serving
Active Time: 15 minutes
Cook Time: 35 minutes
Total Time: 50 minutes

CHOPPED CHICKPEA SALAD VEGGIE BOWL

YIELD: 2 SERVINGS

This is a delicious dish that incorporates chickpea salad. There's lots of roughage, too, that just begs for the simple balsamic dressing.

INGREDIENTS:

Quinoa

½ cup dry quinoa

1 cup vegetable broth

Pinch of salt

Chickpea Salad

1 15-ounce can chickpeas, drained and rinsed

¼ cup vegan mayonnaise

1 tablespoon nutritional yeast

1 tablespoon cider vinegar

½ teaspoon ground mustard

2 scallions, finely sliced

1 teaspoon salt

Pinch of cayenne pepper

Dressing

½ cup extra virgin olive oil

¼ cup balsamic vinegar

To Assemble

3 cups chopped romaine lettuce

½ cup diced purple cabbage

½ cup diced orange bell pepper

INSTRUCTIONS:

Quinoa

1. Place the quinoa in a sieve and rinse well. Combine quinoa, broth, and salt in a small saucepan. Bring to a boil, cover, and reduce to a simmer. Cook for 15 minutes or until the broth is absorbed. Remove from the heat and let set with the cover on for 5 minutes. Remove the lid and fluff out into a small bowl to cool.

Chickpea Salad

2. Place all of the chickpea salad ingredients in a food processor. Pulse four or five times. The chickpeas should be chunky. Remove the blade and stir to make sure the mixture is blended well.

Dressing

3. Mix the oil and vinegar together in a small bowl and set aside.

Assembly

4. Divide the lettuce between two bowls. Lay the vegetables in decorative rows: cabbage, quinoa, bell pepper, and chickpea salad, leaving an edge of romaine lettuce. Serve with the dressing.

Protein: 17 grams per serving
Active Time: 20 minutes
Cook Time: 15 minutes
Total Time: 35 minutes

ROASTED ROOT VEGETABLE SALAD BOWL

YIELD: 2 SERVINGS

Here's the perfect bowl to get a good helping of vegetables. Simply roast a few root vegetables and then chop a few more veggies to create this healthy power bowl. It's perfect with a nutty sweet tahini sauce.

INGREDIENTS:

Roasted Vegetables

1   sweet potato, peeled and chopped into bite-size pieces

1   parsnip, peeled and sliced into ¼-inch rounds

2   carrots, peeled and sliced into ½-inch rounds

2   tablespoons extra virgin olive oil

½   teaspoon salt

Tahini Dressing

¼   cup tahini

1   tablespoon maple syrup

1   tablespoon lemon juice

1   clove garlic

¼   teaspoon salt

Pinch of ground black pepper

3   tablespoons water

To Assemble

¼   cup diced red onion

½   cup chopped red cabbage

9   ounces baby spinach

¼   cup raw shelled hempseed

1   tablespoon chia seeds, black or white

INSTRUCTIONS:

Roasted Vegetables

1. Preheat the oven to 375°F.

2. Place the sweet potatoes, parsnips, and carrots on a baking sheet, keeping them separated. Drizzle the oil over the top and lightly toss, still keeping the vegetables separated. Sprinkle with salt. Bake for 30 to 35 minutes or until they can be pierced with a fork. Set aside.

Tahini Dressing

3. Add all the dressing ingredients to a blender and blend until smooth.

Assembly

4. Prepare the salad bowls by placing half the spinach in the bottom of each bowl. Arrange all the remaining vegetables and hempseed in a circle around the edge of the bowl. Pour half of the dressing in the center of the vegetable round. Sprinkle with the chia seeds.

Protein: 24 grams per serving
Active Time: 15 minutes
Cook Time: 35 minutes
Total Time: 50 minutes

A TOUCH OF THE TROPICS RICE BOWL

YIELD: 2 SERVINGS

There has to be a rice bowl in your repertoire. It's such a good way to enjoy so many different kinds of fruits and veggies. This rice bowl showcases the tastes of the tropics.

INGREDIENTS:

Bowl

1 sweet potato, peeled and chopped into bite-size pieces

1 tablespoon extra virgin olive oil

2 cups jasmine rice, cooked

1 pineapple, peeled, cored, and chopped into bite-size pieces

¼ cup cashews

4 tablespoons raw shelled hempseed

Sweet and Sour Sauce

1 tablespoon cornstarch

½ cup chopped pineapple

¼ cup rice vinegar

⅓ cup light brown sugar

3 tablespoons ketchup

2 teaspoons soy sauce

INSTRUCTIONS:

Sweet Potato

1. Preheat the oven to 425°F.

2. Toss the sweet potato with the oil. Place on a baking sheet and roast for 30 minutes.

3. Remove from the oven and let cool.

Sweet and Sour Sauce

4. Whisk together cornstarch and 1 tablespoon water in a small bowl. Set aside.

5. Add the pineapple and ¼ cup water to a blender. Blend until the mixture is as smooth as possible.

6. Add the pineapple mixture, rice vinegar, brown sugar, ketchup, and soy sauce to a medium saucepan. Bring to a boil over medium-high heat. Stir in the cornstarch mixture and cook until thickened, about a minute. Remove from the heat and set aside while assembling bowls.

Assembly

7. Place rice in the bottom of each bowl. Add rows of pineapple, cashews, hempseed, and sweet potato. Top with the sweet and sour sauce.

Protein: 21 grams per serving
Active Time: 15 minutes
Cook Time: 10 minutes
Total Time: 25 minutes

SOUTHWEST VEGGIE-PACKED SALAD BOWL

YIELD: 2 SERVINGS

Vibrant colors fill this bowl with all the best vegetables associated with the Southwest. Add a small sweet potato and a spicy dressing and you're all set.

INGREDIENTS:

Vegetables

1 small sweet potato, peeled and chopped in bite-size pieces

2 tablespoon extra virgin olive oil, divided

½ cup green lentils

½ cup diced red onion

½ cup diced bell pepper, orange and yellow

½ cup canned kidney beans, drained and rinsed

1 ear corn on the cob, kernels cut off of cob

1 teaspoon salt

Dressing

¼ cup extra virgin olive oil

¼ cup lime juice

2 tablespoons maple syrup

¼ to ½ teaspoon hot sauce

½ teaspoon salt

To Assemble

2 cups mixed lettuce

½ cup grape tomatoes, sliced in half

INSTRUCTIONS:

Vegetables

1. Preheat the oven to 400°F.

2. Place the sweet potato on a baking sheet and sprinkle with 1 tablespoon oil and toss. Roast for about 25 minutes or until you can pierce the sweet potato easily with a fork.

3. While the sweet potato is roasting, rinse the lentils. Add 1 cup water and the lentils to a medium saucepan. Cover, bring to a boil, crack lid, and turn down the heat to medium. Cook about 20 minutes or until the lentils are tender.

4. Meanwhile, heat 1 tablespoon oil in a skillet over medium-high heat. Add the onion and bell pepper and sauté for about 10 to 15 minutes or until the onion is translucent. Add the kidney beans and corn and heat through. Stir in the lentils, sweet potato, salt, and set aside.

Dressing

5. Mix all the ingredients for the dressing and set aside.

Protein: 24 grams per serving
Active Time: 20 minutes
Cook Time: 25 minutes
Total Time: 45 minutes

The High-Protein Vegan Cookbook

Assembly

6. Divide the lettuce between two salad bowls, pulling the lettuce up higher on half of the bowl. Divide the lentil mixture between each bowl, filling up half the bowl. Lay a row of sliced grape tomatoes between the lettuce and vegetable mixture. Serve with the dressing.

SPICED CAULIFLOWER TEMPEH SALAD BOWL

YIELD: 2 SERVINGS

Baked cauliflower comes into its own with some spices added. Marinate tempeh in a slightly tangy dressing, add a little more color and taste contrast, and you'll be in power mode in no time.

INGREDIENTS:

Bowl

1   small head of cauliflower, cut into florets

2   tablespoons extra virgin olive oil

1   teaspoon salt

½   teaspoon ground cumin

¼   teaspoon ground black pepper

Dressing

½   cup vegan mayonnaise

¼   cup unsweetened dairy-free milk

1   teaspoon lemon juice

¼   teaspoon garlic powder

¼   teaspoon onion powder

¼   teaspoon dill weed

Pinch of salt

Pinch of ground black pepper

8   ounces tempeh, sliced into ¼-inch-thick slices and then into small bite-size pieces

8   ounces baby spinach

1   small red onion, cut into bite-size pieces

2   carrots, cut into small matchstick pieces

1   yellow bell pepper, cut into bite-size pieces

INSTRUCTIONS:

Cauliflower

1. Preheat the oven to 400°F.

2. Place the cauliflower florets into a large bowl. Sprinkle with the oil, salt, cumin, and ¼ teaspoon pepper. Toss. Spread out onto a baking sheet and bake for about 25 minutes or until you can easily pierce the cauliflower with a fork. Remove from the oven and set aside.

Dressing

3. While the cauliflower is baking, make the salad dressing. Mix the mayonnaise, milk, lemon juice, garlic and onion powders, dill weed, salt, and pinch of pepper in a small bowl. Place the tempeh in the dressing to marinate while the cauliflower is baking.

Assembly

4. Divide the spinach between two salad bowls. Make a line in the shape of an arc with each vegetable starting with the onion and continuing on with the carrots, cauliflower, and bell pepper. Remove tempeh from the marinade and add it as the final touch to the bowl. Serve with the dressing.

Protein: 20 grams per serving
Active Time: 20 minutes
Cook Time: 15 minutes
Total Time: 35 minutes

EDAMAME AND BROCCOLI RICE BOWL

YIELD: 2 SERVINGS

Tahini sauce pulls this rice-based bowl all together. Each vegetable can stand on its own, but when they mingle with each other, the result is memorable.

INGREDIENTS:

Bowl

½ cup broccoli florets

½ cup edamame, frozen

¼ teaspoon salt

¼ cup peas, frozen or fresh

½ cup chopped yellow bell pepper

Tahini Sauce

¼ cup tahini

1 tablespoon lemon juice

1 tablespoon maple syrup

1 tablespoon tamari

To Assemble

2 cups jasmine rice, cooked

¼ cup sunflower seed kernels

¼ cup raisins

INSTRUCTIONS:

Bowl

1. Add water to a medium saucepan with a steamer insert and bring to a boil. Add the broccoli to the insert and steam over boiling water for 10 minutes. Remove from steamer and set aside.

2. Bring 2 cups water to a boil in a small saucepan and add the edamame and salt. Boil for 5 minutes, adding the peas during the last minute. Drain and set aside.

3. Meanwhile, add 2 tablespoons water to a small skillet and heat over medium-high heat. Add the bell pepper and sauté for 10 minutes. Remove from the heat and set aside.

Tahini Sauce

4. Add all the ingredients plus 5 tablespoons water to a small bowl and blend until smooth.

Assembly

5. Add the rice to the bottom of each bowl. Divide the remaining items in half and add onto the rice in a pinwheel fashion, making sure that the greens don't touch each other for a more pleasing design.

6. Serve with the tahini sauce.

Protein: 20 grams per serving
Active Time: 20 minutes
Cook Time: 30 minutes
Total Time: 50 minutes

CARIBBEAN CHILI

YIELD: 4 SERVINGS

Treat yourself to some spicy chili with a bucketful of veggies. This recipe can be served all year round because of its warmth in the winter and its summer festive vibe.

INGREDIENTS:

- 2 tablespoons coconut oil
- 1 onion, diced
- 1 green pepper, diced
- 3 Roma tomatoes, chopped
- 2 carrots, diced
- 5 ounces tomato paste
- 2 tablespoons chili powder
- 1 teaspoon salt
- 1 teaspoon ground cumin
- ½ teaspoon cinnamon
- ½ teaspoon allspice
- ½ teaspoon dried oregano
- ½ teaspoon cayenne pepper
- ¼ teaspoon garlic powder
- ¼ teaspoon garlic, minced
- ¼ teaspoon ground black pepper
- 1 15-ounce can kidney beans, drained and rinsed
- 1 ear corn, kernels cut from the cob

INSTRUCTIONS:

1. Heat the oil in a large skillet over medium-high heat and add the onion and bell pepper. Sauté until the onion is translucent, about 10 to 15 minutes.

2. Add the tomatoes, carrots, tomato paste, and ½ cup of water. Add the spices and herbs. Bring to a boil, cover, and turn down to simmer for 30 minutes.

3. Add the kidney beans and corn. Cook on a low simmer for another 15 minutes.

Protein: 13 grams per serving
Active Time: 30 minutes
Cook Time: 1 hour
Total Time: 1 hour 30 minutes

MIXED BEANS CHILI

YIELD: 6 SERVINGS

How about some vegan chili that is comforting and full-flavored at the same time? It's made from scratch to warm you, your family, and your home.

INGREDIENTS:

1 pound beans, mixed varieties (you can buy premixed or mix your own)

1 tablespoon extra virgin olive oil

½ cup diced onion

4 cloves garlic, finely chopped

4 cups vegetable broth, more if needed

1 28-ounce can crushed fire-roasted tomatoes

1 8-ounce can tomato sauce

1 6-ounce can tomato paste

2 tablespoons vegan Worcestershire sauce

2 tablespoons chili powder

2 teaspoons ground cumin

1½ teaspoons dried oregano

¼ teaspoon ground cloves

½ teaspoon cayenne pepper

1 teaspoon salt

Protein: 20 grams per serving
Active Time: 10 minutes
Soaking Time: 8 hours
Cook Time: 1 hour 30 minutes
Total Time: 9 hours 40 minutes

INSTRUCTIONS:

The Night Before

1. Rinse the beans and place in a large stockpot. Cover with water by about 3 inches. The beans will swell. Let soak overnight.

The Next Morning

2. Drain the beans and place back into the stockpot.

3. Heat the oil in a large skillet over medium-high heat. Add the onion and sauté until translucent, about 10 to 15 minutes. Add the garlic and sauté another minute. Add this mixture to the beans in the stockpot. Add the vegetable broth, crushed tomatoes, tomato sauce, tomato paste, and Worcestershire sauce. The beans should be covered by a couple of inches of liquid. You can add more broth or water, if needed. Stir well. Add the remaining ingredients and stir well again. Cover and bring to a boil.

4. Remove the lid, turn down the heat, and simmer very low. So low you can barely see the liquid moving. Don't put the lid back on. It becomes much more flavorful with the lid off. If the liquid cooks down to where the beans are not submerged, then add some more broth or water. (If you add more liquid, you'll have to cover again, raise the heat to a boil, and then turn it down immediately and uncover.) Make sure your heat isn't too high. Cook for 1 hour and check the beans. You will want them tender. If they are not done yet, then cook longer. You shouldn't need to cook longer than 1½ hours.

ULTIMATE VEGGIE WRAP WITH KALE PESTO

YIELD: 2 SERVINGS

Pretty in green on the inside and out. Tender broccoli and fresh veggie layers add to the flavorful kale pesto before you roll these up for your first bite.

INGREDIENTS:

Kale Pesto

- ¼ cup raw cashews, soaked at least 2 hours
- 1 cup kale, de-stemmed and coarsely chopped
- 1 clove garlic
- ½ teaspoon salt
- 2 tablespoons nutritional yeast
- 3 tablespoons extra virgin olive oil

Wrap

- ½ cup broccoli florets
- 2 spinach tortillas
- ¼ cup grated carrots
- ¼ cup diced red onion
- ½ yellow bell pepper, diced
- 6 ounces spinach
- 2 tablespoons raw shelled hempseed
- 2 tablespoons sunflower seed kernels

INSTRUCTIONS:

Kale Pesto

1. Place the cashews, kale, garlic, and salt in a small food processor. Process for about 30 seconds. Add the nutritional yeast and oil and process a few more seconds until well blended. Set aside.

Assembly

2. Add water to a medium saucepan with a steamer insert and bring to a boil. Add the broccoli to the insert and steam over boiling water for 10 minutes. Remove from steamer and set aside.

3. Lay out the spinach tortillas. Divide the kale pesto between the two tortillas and spread evenly, leaving about 1 inch around all edges. Divide the remaining ingredients in half and lay out each half next to each other and down the length of each tortilla.

4. Start to roll up snugly, without tearing the tortilla. Cut each tortilla in half and serve.

Protein: 24 grams per serving
Active Time: 30 minutes
Soaking Time: 2 hours
Cook Time: 10 minutes
Total Time: 2 hours 40 minutes

SPROUT SANDWICH WITH TOFU RICOTTA

YIELD: 2 SERVINGS

A nice thick layer of homemade tofu ricotta and sun-dried tomato pesto make a terrific sandwich. Add even more veggies for a unique and delicious lunch.

INGREDIENTS:

Sun-Dried Tomato Pesto

¼ cup baby spinach, packed

2 tablespoons sun-dried tomatoes packed in oil, drained (save the oil)

1 tablespoon pine nuts

1 clove garlic

2 teaspoons nutritional yeast

Pinch of garlic powder

¼ teaspoon salt

1 tablespoon oil or reserved oil from the sun-dried tomatoes

Tofu Ricotta

7 ounces extra-firm tofu, drained, pressed (page 17), and crumbled

1 tablespoon extra virgin olive oil

1 teaspoon cider vinegar

1 teaspoon lemon juice

½ teaspoon garlic powder

½ teaspoon onion powder

To Assemble

4 slices sprouted grain bread

1 cup alfalfa sprouts

1 Roma tomato, sliced

2 slices red onion

Pinch of garlic powder

INSTRUCTIONS:

Sun-Dried Tomato Pesto

1. Place all the pesto ingredients in a small food processor, starting with the spinach. Process until well blended.

Tofu Ricotta

2. Place all the ricotta ingredients in a small food processor. Process until well blended.

Assembly

3. Spread a thick layer of the tofu ricotta on two bread slices. Spread pesto on the other two bread slices. Divide the sprouts, tomato, and onion and place on the ricotta. Top with the pesto slice. Slice each sandwich into fourths in triangle shapes.

Protein: 26 grams per serving
Active Time: 30 minutes
Total Time: 30 minutes

PESTO AND CRISPY TOFU FLATBREAD SANDWICH

YIELD: 2 SERVINGS

Multiple textures and flavors galore make this sandwich a prime target for your regular recipe rotation.

INGREDIENTS:

Tofu

2 ounces extra-firm tofu, drained, pressed (page 17), and cut into 1-inch cubes

¼ cup vegetable broth

1 tablespoon tamari

1 teaspoon onion powder

¼ teaspoon salt

¼ cup cornstarch

Pesto

¼ cup raw cashews, soaked for 1 hour

1 cup basil, packed

1 clove garlic

½ teaspoon salt

2 tablespoons nutritional yeast

3 tablespoons extra virgin olive oil

To Assemble

1 tablespoon coconut oil

¼ cup diced onion

6 mushrooms, sliced

¼ cup hummus

2 slices flatbread

½ cup sunflower sprouts

INSTRUCTIONS:

Tofu

1. Mix together the vegetable broth, tamari, onion powder, and salt in a small bowl. Add the tofu and let marinate at least 1 hour.

2. Preheat the oven to 350°F.

3. Place the cornstarch in a medium bowl.

4. Remove the tofu from the marinade and place on the cornstarch. Toss and then set on a baking sheet. Bake for 30 to 40 minutes. Toss with a spatula every 10 minutes until golden and puffed.

Pesto

5. Place the cashews, basil, garlic, and salt in a small food processor. Process for about 30 seconds. Add the nutritional yeast and olive oil and process a few more seconds until well blended.

Protein: 33 grams per serving
Active Time: 15 minutes
Soaking Time: 1 hour
Cook Time: 40 minutes
Total Time: 1 hour 55 minutes

The High-Protein Vegan Cookbook

Assembly

6. Heat the coconut oil in a skillet over medium-high heat. Add the onions and mushrooms and sauté for about 10 to 15 minutes or until onion is translucent. Remove from the heat.

7. Spread half of the hummus on each flatbread. Spread half of the pesto on each flatbread. Sprinkle half of the tofu, sunflower sprouts, mushrooms, and onion down the center of each flatbread. Fold each flatbread to overlap and secure with decorative picks.

SEITAN AND SUN-DRIED TOMATO PESTO VEGGIE SANDWICH

YIELD: 2 SERVINGS

Thick slices of special seitan and tender cauliflower make the best sandwich when combined with pesto and spinach. After all is encased in a folded flatbread, it simply begs for a bite.

INGREDIENTS:

Cauliflower

1 tablespoon extra virgin olive oil

½ cup cauliflower florets

Pinch of salt

Sun-Dried Tomato Pesto

¼ cup baby spinach, packed

2 tablespoons sun-dried tomatoes packed in oil, drained (save the oil)

1 tablespoon pine nuts

1 clove garlic

2 teaspoons nutritional yeast

Pinch of garlic powder

¼ teaspoon salt

1 tablespoon oil or reserved oil from the sun-dried tomatoes

To Assemble

2 slices flatbread

1 ounce baby spinach

¾ cup Slow Cooker Maple Breakfast Links, sliced (page 276)

2 slices red onion

INSTRUCTIONS:

Cauliflower

1. Preheat the oven to 425°F.

2. Sprinkle the oil on a baking sheet. Lay the cauliflower on the oil and sprinkle with salt. Toss with your hands to get the oil dispersed onto the cauliflower. Bake for 20 minutes or until the cauliflower can be pierced easily with a fork. Remove and set side.

Sun-Dried Tomato Pesto

3. Place all of the pesto ingredients in a small food processor, starting with the spinach. Process until well blended.

Assembly

4. Lay out the flatbreads. Spread half the pesto on each flatbread. Divide the spinach, seitan, cauliflower, and onion between the flatbread slices. Fold each flatbread to overlap and secure with decorative picks.

Protein: 28 grams per serving
Active Time: 20 minutes
Cook Time: 20 minutes
Total Time: 40 minutes

PORTABELLA MUSHROOM GYRO

YIELD: 2 SERVINGS

Big fat marinated portabellas are what dreams are made of. Dripping with flavor and nestled in spinach, just add the best white sauce ever.

INGREDIENTS:

Vegetables

2   large portabella mushroom caps

2   tablespoons vegan Worcestershire sauce

1   teaspoon ground cumin

1   teaspoon maple syrup

½   teaspoon dried oregano

1   tablespoon coconut oil

¼   cup diced red onion

½   red bell pepper, diced large

Fresh White Sauce

½   cup vegan mayonnaise

¼   cup raw shelled hempseeds

1   tablespoon lemon juice

¼   teaspoon dried mint

¼   teaspoon dill weed

To Assemble

2   pita flatbreads

1   ounce baby spinach

INSTRUCTIONS:

Vegetables

1. Remove the stems from the mushrooms and also remove the gills with a spoon. Discard. Slice the mushrooms into thick strips.

2. Mix the Worcestershire sauce, cumin, maple syrup, and oregano in a medium bowl. Lay the mushroom slices in the marinade and let marinate for 10 minutes.

3. Heat the oil in a large skillet over medium-high heat. Add the onion and bell pepper and sauté for 10 minutes. Add the marinated mushroom slices and sauté for 5 more minutes. Remove from the heat and let cool.

Fresh White Sauce

4. Mix all of the Fresh White Sauce ingredients in a small bowl and set aside.

Assembly

5. Lay out a layer of spinach leaves on each flatbread. Spoon the Fresh White Sauce down the center. Lay the mushroom and bell pepper mixture on top. Fold each flatbread to overlap and secure with decorative picks.

Protein: 16 grams per serving
Active Time: 15 minutes
Cook Time: 15 minutes
Total Time: 30 minutes

VEGGIE STUFFED CALZONE

YIELD: 2 SERVINGS

This homemade calzone dough is stuffed with prepared veggies and a little of this and a little of that. Slide it in the oven to bake for a great lunch that you deserve.

INGREDIENTS:

Dough

1   packet dry active yeast

1   tablespoon extra virgin olive oil

¾   teaspoon salt

¾   cup whole wheat pastry flour

1   cup unbleached all-purpose flour

Filling

2   cups broccoli florets

1   tablespoon extra virgin olive oil

1   red bell pepper, diced

1   cup cremini mushrooms

½   cup diced red onion

4   ounces artichoke hearts in water, drained

2   tablespoons chopped walnuts

½   teaspoon dried rosemary

¼   teaspoon salt

¼   teaspoon ground black pepper

½   cup vegan mayonnaise or spread of your choice

2   tablespoons dairy-free milk

2   tablespoons cornmeal

Protein: 21 grams per serving
Active Time: 30 minutes
Rising Time: 90 minutes
Cook Time: 25 minutes
Total Time: 2 hours 25 minutes

INSTRUCTIONS:

Dough

1. Oil the inside of a large bowl and set aside. This is for the dough to rise.

2. Pour ¼ cup warm water (100 to 110°F) in a different large warmed bowl (a microwave can warm the bowl). Stir in the yeast and set aside for 10 minutes. Stir in ¾ cup water, the oil, and the salt. Add the flours and stir until blended. It will not be smooth.

3. Transfer to a floured counter and knead about 4 minutes until smooth, adding a little more flour when you need to keep it from sticking. Slightly sticky is okay. Form into a ball. Place the dough ball in the large greased bowl and turn the dough so that it gets oil on all sides. If you don't do this, you will get a dry crust on the outside of the ball. Cover the bowl and set aside (away from any drafts) until the dough has doubled in size, 40 to 60 minutes.

4. Divide the dough in half. Shape the dough halves into two balls and set on a floured counter. Cover again with a towel and let rise another 20 to 30 minutes.

5. On a lightly floured surface, flatten and push out the dough with your fingers or use a rolling pin to form two circles of the same size, about 10 inches each. One will be the top and one will be the bottom. Cover with a towel again and let rest for 10 to 15 minutes.

Filling

6. Add water to a medium saucepan with a steamer insert and bring to a boil. Add the broccoli to the insert and steam over boiling water for 10 minutes. Remove from steamer and set aside.

7. Heat the oil in a large skillet over medium-high heat. Add the red bell pepper, mushrooms, and onions and sauté for 10 minutes. Add the artichoke hearts, walnuts, rosemary, salt, and pepper and sauté 5 more minutes. Stir in the broccoli and set aside.

Assembly

8. Preheat the oven to 425°F.

9. Uncover the calzone dough. Spread the mayonnaise on one dough round. Next spread the broccoli mixture, leaving about ½ to 1 inch of the edge not covered. Carefully lift the plain dough round and place on the broccoli-covered round. Press and fold the edges over. Cut a few slits in the top of the dough. Brush lightly with milk.

10. Spread the cornmeal on a baking sheet. Carefully lift the calzone onto the baking sheet. Bake for 15 to 18 minutes.

11. Cut the calzone as you would a pizza and serve.

SEITAN SLOPPY JOES

A rich barbecue sauce and enriched seitan make for a much-loved sandwich. Hold it over a plate and have a big bite. Now *that's* good!

INGREDIENTS:

2 cups seitan, crumbled (Slow Cooker Log for Thin Slices and Crumbles, page 280)

8 ounces tomato sauce

⅓ cup organic ketchup

1 tablespoon vegan Worcestershire sauce

2 tablespoons red wine vinegar

2 tablespoons coconut sugar

6 toasted whole wheat buns

INSTRUCTIONS:

Add all of the ingredients except the buns to a large skillet. Bring to a boil, then turn the heat down to medium. Cook for 15 minutes. Serve on the toasted buns.

Protein: 26 grams per serving
Active Time: 10 minutes
Cook Time: 20 minutes
Total Time: 30 minutes

SPICED GREEN LENTIL SANDWICH

YIELD: 8 SERVINGS

Lots of texture and wonderful flavors enhance this spiced-up sandwich. It's one of the best veggie combinations you could ask for.

INGREDIENTS:

1   cup green lentils

1   small potato, to equal about ½ cup mashed potato

½   cup chopped onion

1   carrot, finely chopped in a processor

¾   cup old-fashioned oats

½   cup pepitas or sunflower seed kernels

1   tablespoon hempseed, toasted in shell

1   cup breadcrumbs

4   tablespoons tamari

1   teaspoon ground ginger

1½ teaspoons smoked paprika

½   teaspoon salt

¼   teaspoon ground black pepper

1   tablespoon coconut oil

8   sandwich buns

INSTRUCTIONS:

1. Place 2 cups water and the lentils in a large sauce-pan. Cover and bring to a boil. Turn down to low and cook for 20 minutes. Drain off remaining liquid from the lentils, if any. Set the lentils aside.

2. Pierce the potato a couple of times with a sharp knife. Wrap in a damp paper towel. Set in the microwave and cook on high for 4 minutes or until you can pinch the potato easily. Peel the potato and mash well. Set aside.

3. Heat 2 tablespoons water in a skillet over medium-high heat. Add the onion and sauté for 10 minutes. Remove from the heat.

4. Add the lentils, potato, onion, and the remainder of the ingredients to a large bowl (excluding the oil and the buns). Mix well. Form eight patties to the size of your sandwich buns.

5. Heat the oil in a frying pan and fry the lentil pat-ties on each side without crowding.

6. Spread the buns with all your favorite condiments and any other toppings of your choice.

7. You may also freeze extra patties for future meals.

Protein: 14 grams per serving
Active Time: 20 minutes
Cook Time: 10 minutes
Total Time: 30 minutes

YIELD: 6 SERVINGS

Treat yourself to one of the most popular sandwiches out there. An added bonus is that this version has little bits of carrots and corn.

INGREDIENTS:

1½ cups breadcrumbs, fresh

2 tablespoons chia seeds or ground chia seeds

2 tablespoons coconut oil, divided

1 cup diced yellow onion

½ cup finely diced carrot

1 ear of corn, kernels cut from the cob, or 1 8-ounce can corn, drained

½ teaspoon dried oregano

2 teaspoons chili powder

¼ teaspoon ground cumin

1 teaspoon salt

2 cloves garlic, finely diced

1 28-ounce can black beans, drained and rinsed

¼ cup sunflower seed kernels

2 tablespoons raw shelled hempseed

6 whole wheat buns

Condiments and toppings of your choice

Protein: 22 grams per serving
Active Time: 15 minutes
Cook Time: 20 minutes
Total Time: 35 minutes

INSTRUCTIONS:

1. Make your breadcrumbs using any leftover bread that you have. I used whole wheat but you could use sourdough and whatever else you prefer. Place bread in a food processor and process until the bread is a finely ground texture. Set aside. If you have any leftover breadcrumbs, they can be frozen for 6 months.

2. Mix the chia seeds with 6 tablespoons water and set aside.

3. Heat 1 tablespoon oil in a large skillet, add the onion and carrot, and sauté about 10 minutes. Add the corn and cook another 3 minutes. Add the spices and garlic to the onion and cook another minute.

4. Pat the black beans dry. You want to make sure they aren't wet when mashing and adding to the rest of ingredients. In a large bowl, add the black beans and mash with a potato masher or the back of a fork. You could pulse them in a food processor instead, but not too fine. Stir in the chia seed mixture. Mix in the onion mixture, breadcrumbs, sunflower seed kernels, and hempseed.

5. Make into six patties. At this point you can freeze the patties, before frying.

6. Fry the patties in 1 tablespoon medium-hot oil until browned on each side.

7. Serve on the whole wheat buns with your favorite toppings.

DOUBLE-DECKER RED QUINOA SANDWICH

YIELD: 3 SERVINGS

A little preparation and a food processor takes you a long way to this satisfying sandwich. Red quinoa has the same nutty taste and nutrition of its pearly cousin, and it's just darn pretty.

INGREDIENTS:

½ cup red quinoa

1 cup vegetable broth

4 large portabella mushroom caps

2 tablespoons coconut oil, divided

¼ cup finely chopped onion

½ cup raw pecans

2 green spring onions, chopped

2 teaspoons rice wine vinegar

1 teaspoon garlic powder

2 tablespoons nutritional yeast

2 tablespoons raw shelled hempseed

¼ cup flour

3 whole wheat burger buns

Toppings and condiments: lettuce, tomatoes, red onion, mustard, dairy-free spicy mayo

---

Protein: 24 grams per serving
Active Time: 20 minutes
Cook Time: 35 minutes
Total Time: 55 minutes

INSTRUCTIONS:

1. Place the quinoa in a sieve and rinse well. Combine the quinoa and broth in a small saucepan. Bring to a boil, cover, and reduce to a simmer. Cook for 10 to 15 minutes or until the broth is absorbed. Remove from the heat and let set with the cover on for 5 minutes.

2. Remove the gills from the mushrooms and discard. Chop up the mushroom caps.

3. Heat 1 tablespoon oil in a large skillet. Add the onion and mushrooms and sauté for 10 minutes. Add the pecans and sauté for 5 more minutes. Remove from the heat and let cool.

4. Add the mushroom mixture, green onion, and vinegar to a food processor. Process until very fine. It will not be smooth.

5. Transfer to a large bowl and add the quinoa, garlic powder, nutritional yeast, hempseed, and flour. Mix until well blended. Form into six patties the size of the burger buns.

6. Heat remaining oil in a large skillet and fry one patty at a time so that you can flip it easily. Fry until golden brown on each side.

7. Assemble the double deckers: Lay down the bottom of the bun, add mustard, lettuce, patty, red onion, lettuce, dairy-free spicy mayo, patty, dairy-free spicy mayo, tomatoes, and top of bun.

LOADED CHICKPEA SALAD SANDWICH

YIELD: 8 SERVINGS

Here's a complete meal for your whole family. It's a big batch, it's quick to prepare, and it keeps great in the fridge or freezer.

INGREDIENTS:

- 2 15-ounce cans chickpeas, drained and rinsed
- 2 15-ounce cans pinto beans, drained and rinsed
- 2 tablespoons raw shelled hempseed
- 1 tablespoon vegan mayonnaise (add another tablespoon if you like it better that way)
- 1 tablespoon Dijon mustard (add another tablespoon if desired)
- 2 tablespoons lemon juice (optional)
- ¼ teaspoon garlic powder
- ¼ teaspoon paprika
- ½ teaspoon salt
- ¼ teaspoon ground black pepper
- 16 slices whole wheat bread or sprouted grain bread
- 2 avocados, sliced
- 2 ounces baby spinach

INSTRUCTIONS:

1. In a large bowl, add the beans and mash. Leave a bit chunky, not completely mashed. Add the remaining ingredients except the bread, avocado, and spinach. Mix well.

2. Spread on the bread slices. Add the avocado slices and spinach. You can also keep any extra chickpea salad in your fridge for up to 5 days.

Protein: 21 grams per serving
Active Time: 15 minutes
Total Time: 15 minutes

FRESH VEGGIE SEITAN PITA POCKET

YIELD: 2 SERVINGS

Fresh vegetables and tender seitan fill up these pita pockets for a memorable lunch.

INGREDIENTS:

1   tablespoon extra virgin olive oil

1   cup Steamed Seitan Smoky Nuggets, sliced thick (page 283)

½   cup broccoli florets, chopped small

½   cup diced red bell pepper

½   cup diced cucumber

1   carrot, grated

4   ounces artichoke hearts in water, drained

2   pita pockets

¼   cup dairy-free mayonnaise

1   ounce baby spinach

INSTRUCTIONS:

1. Heat the oil in a large skillet over medium-high heat. Add the seitan, broccoli, and bell pepper and cook over medium heat for 3 minutes. Add the cucumber, carrot, and artichoke hearts. Stir and cook for 1 minute. Take off the heat.

2. Cut the pita pockets in half and spread half the mayonnaise into both halves of each pocket. Add a few leaves of baby spinach and then spoon a quarter of the seitan mixture into each of the four pocket halves.

Protein: 35 grams per serving
Active Time: 15 minutes
Cook Time: 5 minutes
Total Time: 20 minutes

BROCCOLI SPINACH STUFFED BAGUETTE

YIELD: 2 SERVINGS

Broccoli and spinach are added to a warm gooey cashew cheese. Fill up a hollowed-out baguette and it's a feast.

INGREDIENTS:

Vegetables

2   cups broccoli florets

1   tablespoon extra virgin olive oil

2   cloves garlic, finely diced

5   ounces baby spinach, chopped, with the long stems cut away and discarded

Cashew Cheese

½   cup raw cashews, soaked 1 hour and drained

1   cup water

1½ tablespoons nutritional yeast

4   tablespoons tapioca starch

½   teaspoon salt

½   teaspoon garlic powder

To Assemble

1   baguette

1   ounce grape tomatoes, sliced thin

2   tablespoons raw shelled hempseed

Protein: 31 grams per serving
Active Time: 45 minutes
Soaking Time: 1 hour
Cook Time: 25 minutes
Total Time: 2 hours 10 minutes

INSTRUCTIONS:

Vegetables

1. Add water to a medium saucepan with a steamer insert and bring to a boil. Add the broccoli to the insert and steam over boiling water for 10 minutes. Remove from steamer and set aside.

2. Heat the oil in a large skillet over medium-high heat. Use a skillet that has a lid. Add the garlic and cook for 1 minute. Add the spinach, toss, and cook for 1 minute. Cover and let sit for 2 minutes.

3. Add the broccoli and spinach to a large bowl.

Cashew Cheese

4. Add all of the cashew cheese ingredients to a blender and blend until completely smooth.

5. Pour into a small saucepan and bring heat up to medium high. Keep cooking and stirring until it goes through its thickening process and becomes a gooey, cheesy sauce. This takes 5 to 10 minutes.

6. Add to the bowl with the broccoli mixture. Stir well.

Assembly

7. Cut off the top of the baguette and scoop out some of the bread from the center using a spoon. Make sure you leave an edge of bread in the shell to help hold the filling.

8. Spoon the broccoli-cheese mixture down the center of the baguette. Top with sliced grape tomatoes and sprinkle with hempseed. Cut in half. You could also cut into slices and serve as an appetizer.

TORTA DE SEITAN AND VEGGIES

YIELD: 4 SERVINGS

It will be hard to keep your fork out of the skillet when this spicy mix is being prepared. Fill up those rolls and have a great lunch.

INGREDIENTS:

1 tablespoon coconut oil

½ cup diced red onion

1 green bell pepper, diced

2 cloves garlic, minced

½ teaspoon dried oregano

½ teaspoon ground cumin

4 Steamed Seitan Chipotle Links (page 284)

1 15-ounce can black beans, drained and rinsed

2 sub rolls

1 cup salsa

Romaine lettuce, sliced and chopped

INSTRUCTIONS:

1. Heat the oil in a large skillet over medium-high heat. Add the onion and bell pepper and sauté for 10 to 15 minutes or until onion is translucent. Add the garlic, oregano, and cumin and cook for 1 minute. Tear the seitan into chunks and drop into the skillet. Add the black beans. Stir and cook over medium heat for 5 minutes or until seitan is heated through.

2. Cut each roll in half and scoop out some of the bread center. Spread a layer of salsa on the bread and sprinkle on some chopped romaine lettuce. Fill up with black bean and seitan mixture.

Protein: 31 grams per serving
Active Time: 45 minutes
Cook Time: 25 minutes
Total Time: 1 hour 10 minutes

SPROUTED GRAIN SPICY SEITAN SANDWICH

YIELD: 6 SERVINGS

This super simple sandwich stars tender patties from an Instant Pot or pressure cooker. Premake the seitan and keep in the fridge or freezer for a super fast lunch.

INGREDIENTS:

- 1 tablespoon coconut oil
- 6 Pressure Cooker Tender Patties (page 286)
- 6 sprouted grain English muffins, sliced open
- Condiments of your choice, such as dairy-free chipotle mayo and horseradish mustard
- 1 avocado, sliced
- 6 slices red onion

INSTRUCTIONS:

1. Heat the oil in a large skillet over medium-high heat and fry the patties until just golden on each side.

2. While the patties are in the skillet, toast the English muffins. Layer the toast with mayo, mustard, avocado, patty, and onion.

Protein: 15 grams per serving
Active Time: 5 minutes
Cook Time: 10 minutes
Total Time: 15 minutes

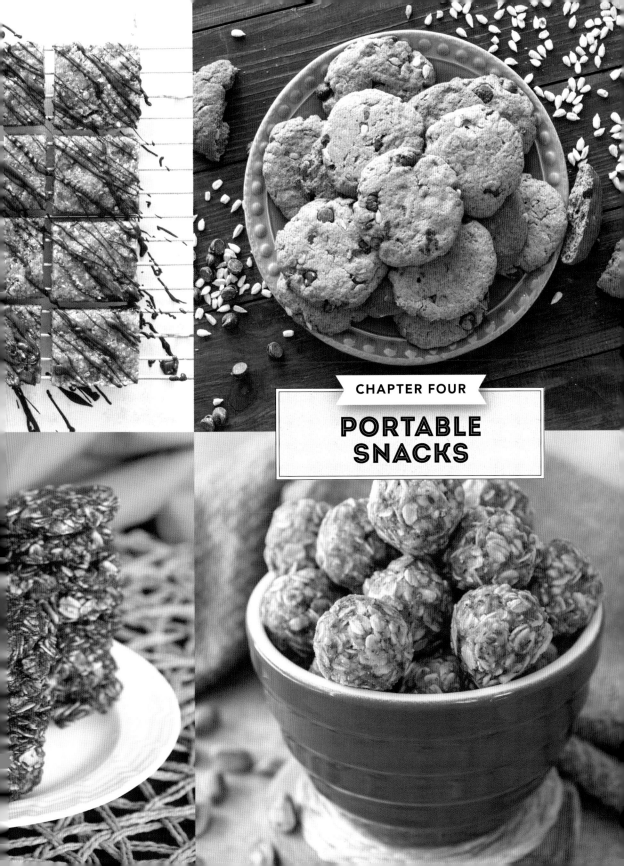

CHAPTER FOUR

PORTABLE SNACKS

AMAZING LENTIL ENERGY BALLS

YIELD: 9 SERVINGS

What?! Lentil balls as a sweet protein snack, you say? Yes, it's possible. They're sweetened just right—try them once and you'll be craving them forever. No kidding!

INGREDIENTS:

½ cup lentils

½ cup dairy-free chocolate chips

2 cups quick-cooking oats

¼ cup sunflower seed kernels

¼ cup raw shelled hempseed

¼ cup unsweetened shredded coconut

½ cup almond butter

½ cup maple syrup

INSTRUCTIONS:

1. Rinse and drain the lentils. Place 1 cup water and the lentils in a medium-large saucepan. Bring to a boil over high heat. When the water comes to a boil, turn down to medium high and cook for 20 to 25 minutes or until the lentils are tender. All the water should be absorbed. Set aside to cool.

2. Add the chocolate chips, oats, sunflower seeds, hempseed, and coconut in a large bowl. Mix in the cooled lentils. Add almond butter and maple syrup. Mix well. Form into thirty-six balls and place in a glass container with a lid.

3. Refrigerate for about 30 minutes. Store in the refrigerator for up to 5 days or freeze for up to 6 months.

Protein: 12 grams per serving (4 balls)
Active Time: 15 minutes
Refrigerator Time: 30 minutes
Cook Time: 25 minutes
Total Time: 1 hour 10 minutes

MIXED BAG CHOCOLATE WALNUT PROTEIN BARS

YIELD: 8 SERVINGS

Everything but the kitchen sink goes into this recipe. The long slim bars will have you happily chewing your way to protein enrichment on your way out the door.

INGREDIENTS:

3   tablespoons peanut butter

3   tablespoons maple syrup

1½ tablespoons coconut oil

1   tablespoon ground chia seeds

1¼ cups quick-cooking oats

½   cup walnuts

½   cup dairy-free chocolate chips

⅓   cup coconut sugar

¼   cup raw shelled hempseed

3   tablespoons protein powder

½   teaspoon ground cinnamon

¼   teaspoon salt

INSTRUCTIONS:

1. Preheat the oven to 350°F.

2. Prepare an 8-inch square baking dish with parchment paper coming up on the sides on two opposite ends. Not over the top, just the sides. This makes for easier removal.

3. Add the peanut butter, maple syrup, and coconut oil to a small saucepan. Heat to melt the peanut butter and stir well. Take off heat and let cool a bit.

4. Mix the ground chia seeds and 3 tablespoons water in a small bowl and set aside.

5. Add the oats, walnuts, chocolate chips, sugar, hempseed, protein powder, cinnamon, and salt to a large bowl. Mix well. Add the chia mixture and peanut butter mixture to the bowl of dry ingredients and mix well.

6. Pour the mixture into the prepared dish and press down with your fingers to make the mix firm and pressed into all corners.

7. Bake for 30 to 35 minutes. The bars will get harder as they cool, so don't overbake.

8. Let cool on a wire rack. To remove, grab hold of the extra parchment paper on the opposite ends of the dish and lift. Place on a cutting board and slice into bars that are about 2 inches wide and then in half at 4 inches long.

Protein: 9 grams per serving
Active Time: 20 minutes
Cook Time: 35 minutes
Total Time: 55 minutes

The High-Protein Vegan Cookbook

PEANUT BUTTER SNACK SQUARES

YIELD: 8 SERVINGS

A double peanut whammy is served up in this recipe. All is sweetened with whipped coconut sugar and dates.

INGREDIENTS:

- ½ cup coconut sugar
- 1 cup creamy peanut butter
- 1 teaspoon vanilla extract
- ¾ cup whole wheat flour
- ¼ cup garbanzo flour
- 1 teaspoon baking soda
- ½ teaspoon baking powder
- 1 cup old-fashioned oats
- ½ cup dairy-free milk
- ½ cup peanuts
- ½ cup dates, pitted and chopped small

INSTRUCTIONS:

1. Preheat the oven to 350°F. Lightly grease an 8-inch square baking dish.

2. Mix the sugar and peanut butter with a hand or stand mixer on medium speed for 5 minutes. Mix in the vanilla. Add the flours, baking soda, and baking powder and mix on medium speed. Add the oats and mix for a few seconds. This will be stiff. Add the milk and mix on medium until just combined.

3. Fold in the peanuts and dates and make sure everything is well incorporated.

4. You can use your hands to press the dough lightly into the prepared dish. Bake for 15 to 20 minutes or until lightly golden brown.

5. Place on a wire rack to cool. Cut into sixteen squares and store in the refrigerator.

Protein: 14 grams per serving (2 squares)
Active Time: 10 minutes
Cook Time: 20 minutes
Total Time: 30 minutes

PACKED PEANUT OATMEAL COOKIES

YIELD: 12 SERVINGS

Peanuts, oats, and dairy-free cream cheese are just the beginning of making a classic cookie that's packed with protein. What's more, they hardly take any time to make!

INGREDIENTS:

1   tablespoon chia seeds or ground chia seeds

1⅓ cups whole wheat flour

1   teaspoon baking powder

1½ cups old-fashioned oats

2   tablespoons vanilla protein powder

½   cup dairy-free butter

1   cup coconut sugar

½   cup dairy-free cream cheese, softened

1   teaspoon vanilla extract

1   banana

1   cup peanuts, chopped

INSTRUCTIONS:

1. Preheat the oven to 400°F. Cut parchment paper to fit on a baking sheet. Set aside.

2. Mix the chia seeds with 3 tablespoons water and set aside.

3. Add the flour, baking powder, oats, and protein powder to a large bowl. Set aside.

4. Add the butter and sugar to the bowl of a stand mixer. Cream on medium-low speed for 5 minutes. Add the cream cheese and mix well. Turn off the beater and add the prepared chia seed mixture, vanilla, and banana. Mix well on medium speed. Add the dry ingredients and peanuts and keep mixing until just combined.

5. Spoon dollops on a cookie sheet 2 inches apart and flatten with the bottom of a glass to about ½-inch thick. Bake for 11 minutes.

6. Cool on a wire rack.

Protein: 8 grams per serving (2 cookies)
Active Time: 15 minutes
Cook Time: 11 minutes
Total Time: 26 minutes

The High-Protein Vegan Cookbook

RICH CHOCOLATE ENERGY COOKIES

YIELD: 12 SERVINGS

These rich energy cookies are big and chewy, and a wonderful variety of ingredients goes into them. They won't stay in your cookie jar for long.

INGREDIENTS:

½ cup dairy-free butter, softened

1 cup coconut sugar

1 tablespoon chia seeds or ground chia seeds

2 cups (12 ounces) dairy-free chocolate chips, divided

1 tablespoon instant coffee

1¼ cups whole wheat flour

½ teaspoon baking soda

1 teaspoon baking powder

½ teaspoon salt

2 tablespoons raw shelled hempseed

1 cup walnuts, chopped

INSTRUCTIONS:

1. Preheat the oven to 350°F. Cut parchment paper to fit on a baking sheet. Set aside.

2. Add the butter and sugar to the bowl of a stand mixer. Cream on medium speed for 5 minutes or until light and fluffy.

3. Mix the chia seeds with 3 tablespoons water and set aside.

4. Melt ½ cup of the chocolate chips in a microwave or in a double boiler. Set aside to cool a bit.

5. Boil 2 tablespoons water and add instant coffee. Set aside to cool.

6. Add flour, baking soda, baking powder, and salt to a bowl. Mix well by hand.

7. Add the prepared chia seed mixture and melted chocolate to the bowl of the stand mixer. Mix well on medium speed. Add the flour mixture and keep mixing until just combined. Remove the mixing bowl and fold in the remaining chocolate chips, hempseed, and walnuts. Mix well.

8. Drop on the prepared cookie sheet by large, heaping tablespoons, 2 inches apart, and flatten slightly. Bake for 12 minutes.

9. Cool on a wire rack.

Protein: 6½ grams per serving (2 cookies)
Active Time: 15 minutes
Cook Time: 15 minutes
Total Time: 30 minutes

ORANGE CRANBERRY POWER COOKIES

YIELD: 12 SERVINGS

Mild fruit flavors blend perfectly in this sweet cookie dough. You'll feel like celebrating when you bite into one of these lightly crispy cookies.

INGREDIENTS:

1 cup dairy-free butter, softened

1 cup coconut sugar

⅓ cup orange juice

2 teaspoons organic vanilla extract

1½ cups whole wheat flour

2 tablespoons protein powder

1 teaspoon baking powder

¼ teaspoon baking soda

1 cup old-fashioned oats

1 cup dairy-free chocolate chips

1 cup walnuts, chopped

1 cup dried cranberries

INSTRUCTIONS:

1. Preheat the oven to 375°F.

2. Beat the butter and sugar together in the bowl of a stand mixer. Add the orange juice and vanilla extract. Mix well.

3. Add flour, protein powder, baking powder, and baking soda to a medium bowl. Mix and add to the wet mixture. Mix on medium speed until well blended. Add the oats, chocolate chips, walnuts, and cranberries. Mix on low.

4. Drop heaping tablespoons about 2 inches apart on an ungreased baking sheet. These are big cookies. They spread out to 3 to 4 inches in diameter. Bake for 10 to 11 minutes.

5. Cool a minute and then transfer to a wire rack to cool completely.

Protein: 6 grams per serving (2 cookies)
Active Time: 15 minutes
Cook Time: 10 minutes
Total Time: 25 minutes

The High-Protein Vegan Cookbook

CHOCOLATE CHIP BANANA BREAD PROTEIN COOKIES

YIELD: 12 SERVINGS

These protein-rich cookies have a high fiber content that fills you up and helps keep you feeling satisfied. They taste delicious, too!

INGREDIENTS:

- 2 tablespoons chia seeds or ground chia seeds
- 1 cup whole wheat flour
- ½ cup almond flour
- ½ cup flaxseed meal
- 2 tablespoons protein powder
- ½ teaspoon baking soda
- ½ teaspoon salt
- ¾ cup dairy-free butter
- ⅔ cup coconut sugar
- ⅓ cup organic light brown sugar, packed
- 1 teaspoon vanilla extract
- ½ cup banana, mashed (1 medium banana)
- 1 cup dairy-free chocolate chips

INSTRUCTIONS:

1. Preheat the oven to 350°F. Cut parchment paper to fit on a baking sheet. Set aside.

2. Mix the chia seeds with 6 tablespoons water and set aside.

3. Add both flours, the flaxseed, protein powder, baking soda, and salt to a large bowl. Set aside.

4. Add butter and both sugars to the bowl of a stand mixer. Mix on medium speed for 5 minutes. Turn off beater and add the prepared chia seed mixture, vanilla, and banana. Mix well on medium speed. Add the dry ingredients and keep mixing until just combined. Remove the mixing bowl and fold in the chocolate chips.

5. Place heaping tablespoons on a cookie sheet 2 inches apart and flatten with the bottom of a glass to about ½ inch thick. Bake for 12 minutes.

6. Cool on a wire rack.

Protein: 6 grams per serving (2 cookies)
Active Time: 15 minutes
Cook Time: 15 minutes
Total Time: 30 minutes

CHOCOLATE CAKE MUNCH COOKIES

YIELD: 12 SERVINGS

Big, fat, and very chocolaty cookies are on the menu for today. Cake-like on the inside, they'll satisfy your cookie cravings any day.

INGREDIENTS:

- ½ cup dairy-free butter, softened
- 1 cup coconut sugar
- 1 tablespoon chia seeds or ground chia seeds
- ¾ cup soy milk
- 1 teaspoon vanilla
- 2 cups whole wheat flour
- ¼ cup protein powder
- 1 teaspoon baking powder
- ½ teaspoon baking soda
- ½ teaspoon salt
- ½ cup cocoa powder
- 1 cup walnuts, chopped

INSTRUCTIONS:

1. Add butter and sugar to the bowl of a stand mixer. Mix on medium speed for 5 minutes.

2. Meanwhile, mix the chia seeds with 3 tablespoons water.

3. Add the chia mixture, milk, and vanilla to the butter and mix well at medium speed.

4. Add the flour, protein powder, baking powder, baking soda, salt, and cocoa to a medium bowl. Mix well.

5. Turn mixer on medium and slowly add the dry mixture. Add the walnuts and mix at low speed until combined. Place the mixture in the refrigerator from one hour to overnight.

6. About 15 minutes before you're ready to bake the cookies, preheat the oven to 400°F. Cut parchment paper to fit on a baking sheet. Set aside.

7. Drop heaping tablespoons onto prepared cookie sheet, 2 inches apart. Roll into balls and then flatten by about half with the bottom of a measuring cup or some other strong material. They bake up thick. Bake for 8 minutes.

8. Cool on a wire rack.

Protein: 7 grams per serving (2 cookies)
Active Time: 10 minutes
Refrigerator Time: 1 hour
Cook Time: 10 minutes
Total Time: 1 hour 20 minutes

CHOCOLATE SUNFLOWER PROTEIN COOKIES

YIELD: 12 SERVINGS

Sunflower seeds add a surprise texture to these softly crunchy chocolate chip cookies. Bake a few dozen for your cookie jar and your tummy.

INGREDIENTS:

1   cup dairy-free butter

¾   cup plus 2 tablespoons coconut sugar

2   tablespoons ground chia seeds

2¼ cups whole wheat pastry flour

¼   cup protein powder

1   teaspoon baking soda

½   teaspoon baking powder

¼   teaspoon salt

1   teaspoon vanilla extract

1   cup dairy-free chocolate chips

¼   cup sunflower seed kernels

INSTRUCTIONS:

1. Preheat the oven to 375°F. Cut parchment paper to fit on a baking sheet. Set aside.

2. Add the butter and sugar to the bowl of stand mixer and mix together on medium-low speed for 5 minutes.

3. Meanwhile, mix ground chia seeds with 6 table-spoons water and set aside.

4. Mix together the flour, protein powder, baking soda, baking powder, and salt in a medium bowl.

5. Add the vanilla and chia mixture to the butter mixture. Mix until well blended. Mix in the flour mixture a little at a time. On low speed, mix in the chocolate chips and sunflower seeds.

6. Form into round balls and set on the prepared baking sheet about 2 inches apart. Flatten to about ½ inch thick. Bake for 8 to 9 minutes.

7. Cool on a wire rack.

Protein: 7 grams per serving (2 cookies)
Active Time: 15 minutes
Cook Time: 10 minutes
Total Time: 25 minutes

PEANUT BUTTER CHOCOLATE SEED BALLS

YIELD: 16 SERVINGS

Here are some perfect little bites that only have five ingredients. The delicious result gives you a nice firm ball. Simple and fast!

INGREDIENTS:

16 ounces dairy-free chocolate chips

½ cup creamy peanut butter

½ cup raw shelled hempseed

½ cup unsweetened shredded coconut

1 cup sunflower seed kernels, pulsed fine in a mini food processor, divided

INSTRUCTIONS:

1. Melt the chocolate in a double boiler. Stir in the peanut butter and blend well. Take off of the the heat and mix in the hempseed, shredded coconut, and ½ cup sunflower seeds. Refrigerate until the dough is firm enough to use a small cookie scoop, about 30 minutes.

2. Remove the dough from the refrigerator and scoop out forty-eight balls. You can roll them into smoother balls with the palms of your hands. While they are still warm from rolling, roll them in the remaining pulsed sunflower seeds.

3. These will keep in the fridge for about 3 weeks and in the freezer for about 6 months.

Protein: 7 grams per serving (3 balls)
Active Time: 15 minutes
Refrigerator Time: 30 minutes
Cook Time: 25 minutes
Total Time: 1 hour 10 minutes

The High-Protein Vegan Cookbook

PROTEIN POWER PISTACHIO BITES

YIELD: 18 BALLS

Who doesn't like pistachios? You can have these bites at a moment's notice, for yourself or friends. They're easy to pack along, too.

INGREDIENTS:

½ cup old-fashioned oats

½ cup almond butter

¼ cup maple syrup

⅓ cup oat bran

⅓ cup flaxseed meal

⅓ cup pistachios, ground

1 tablespoon raw shelled hempseed

INSTRUCTIONS:

1. Add all the ingredients to a large bowl and mix well.

2. Roll into eighteen balls.

Protein: 6 grams per serving (2 balls)
Active Time: 15 minutes
Total Time: 15 minutes

NO-BAKE
CEREAL DATE BARS

YIELD: 16 BARS

Layers of crunchy goodness are filled with so many wonderful sweet flavors. Not too sweet, though—these bars have just the right contrast and balance.

INGREDIENTS:

2 cups granola cereal

2 tablespoons flaxseed meal

2 tablespoons protein powder

½ cup peanuts, chopped

½ cup dates, chopped small

½ cup almond butter

½ cup brown rice syrup

¼ cup maple syrup

INSTRUCTIONS:

1. Line an 8-inch square baking dish with parchment paper and come up about 3 inches on opposite sides. This will act as a handle to remove the bars from the pan.

2. Combine the cereal, flaxseed meal, protein powder, peanuts, and dates in a large bowl.

3. In a small saucepan, add the almond butter and both syrups. Bring to a boil and cook to the hard ball stage, 260°F, on a candy thermometer. Quickly stir into the cereal mixture and then spread into the prepared dish. It will cool quickly, so you can use your fingertips to press down into the dish as evenly as possible. Refrigerate for at least 30 minutes.

4. Grab the "handles" of the parchment paper and lift out of the dish. Place on a cutting board and slice into sixteen squares.

Protein: 9 grams per serving (2 bars)
Active Time: 20 minutes
Cook Time: 15 minutes
Refrigerator Time: 30 minutes
Total Time: 1 hour 5 minutes

TROPICAL LEMON PROTEIN BITES

YIELD: 24 BALLS

You have to have a lemon treat in your bag of tricks. Easy to make, these balls don't fall apart or make any kind of a mess.

INGREDIENTS:

1¾ cups cashews

¼   cup coconut flour

¼   cup unsweetened shredded coconut

3   tablespoons raw shelled hempseed

3   tablespoons maple syrup

3   tablespoons fresh lemon juice

INSTRUCTIONS:

1. Place the cashews in a food processor and process until very fine. Add the rest of the ingredients and process until well blended. Dump the mixture into a large bowl.

2. Take a clump of the dough and squeeze it into a ball. Keep squeezing and working it a few times until a ball is formed and solid.

Protein: 8 grams per serving (2 balls)
Active Time: 20 minutes
Total Time: 20 minutes

CHERRY CHOCOLATE HEMP BALLS

YIELD: 24 BALLS

Take a gander down this list of ingredients. Every nut, grain, fruit, and seed included here just makes me happy. They blend so well together, and they freeze perfectly, too.

INGREDIENTS:

1   cup old-fashioned oats

½   cup unsweetened shredded coconut

½   cup dried cherries, chopped

½   cup pistachios, chopped

⅓   cup dairy-free chocolate chips

⅓   cup peanut butter

¼   cup maple syrup

¼   cup raw shelled hempseed

INSTRUCTIONS:

1.   Add all of the ingredients to a large bowl. Mix well with a sturdy wooden spoon. Roll into 24 balls.

2.   Store in the refrigerator for up to 5 days or freeze for up to 6 months.

Protein: 10 grams per serving (2 balls)
Active Time: 20 minutes
Total Time: 20 minutes

PROTEIN PEANUT BUTTER BALLS

YIELD: 24 BALLS

Here's an easy and healthy treat that you can pop in your mouth any time of the day. Energy-packed with only six ingredients!

INGREDIENTS:

½ cup creamy peanut butter

½ cup maple syrup

½ cup powdered soy milk, non-GMO

¼ cup flaxseed meal

½ cup coconut flour

¼ cup peanuts, chopped fine

INSTRUCTIONS:

1. Place the peanut butter and maple syrup in a medium bowl. Mix well. Add the powdered soy milk, flaxseed meal, and coconut flour. Mix well and roll into 24 balls. Lightly roll each ball in the chopped peanuts.

2. Store in the refrigerator for up to 2 weeks.

Protein: 10 grams per serving (2 balls)
Active Time: 20 minutes
Total Time: 20 minutes

OVER-THE-TOP BARS TO GO

YIELD: 16 SQUARES

Not only are these bars gorgeous, but they travel really well, too. The ingredients are fun because they contain just about every nut and seed that you can think of.

INGREDIENTS:

1½ cups old-fashioned oats

½ cup pecans

½ cup pistachios

½ cup cashews

½ cup dried cranberries

¼ cup dates, pitted and chopped

¼ cup sunflower seed kernels

¼ cup pepitas

2 tablespoons raw shelled hempseed

½ cup peanut butter

½ cup brown rice syrup

3 tablespoons maple syrup

INSTRUCTIONS:

1. Line an 8-inch square baking dish with parchment paper and come up about 3 inches on opposite sides. This will act as a handle to remove the bars from the dish.

2. Mix all the ingredients except the peanut butter and the syrups together in a large bowl. Add the peanut butter and start to mix in with a wooden spoon, and then use your hands to mix and pinch so that the peanut butter is well incorporated into the dry ingredients.

3. Add the brown rice syrup and maple syrup to a small saucepan. Bring to a boil and cook to hard ball stage, 260°F, on a candy thermometer. Pour the syrups over the oat mixture and stir well. Then quickly spread the mixture into the prepared dish. It will cool quickly, so you can use your fingertips to press down into the dish as evenly as possible. You can also use the bottom of a measuring cup to press down firmly. Refrigerate for at least 30 minutes.

4. Grab the "handles" of the parchment paper and lift out of the dish. Place on a cutting board and slice into sixteen squares.

Protein: 13 grams per serving (2 squares)
Active Time: 20 minutes
Refrigerator Time: 30 minutes
Cook Time: 15 minutes
Total Time: 1 hour 5 minutes

The High-Protein Vegan Cookbook

RAW DATE CHOCOLATE BALLS

YIELD: 24 BALLS

These perfect little bites are made with the best variety of ingredients. They are sweet, crunchy, and chocolaty.

INGREDIENTS:

¾ cup sunflower seed kernels, ground

½ cup dates, pitted, chopped well

½ cup walnuts, chopped

½ cup unsweetened cacao powder

½ cup maple syrup

½ cup creamy almond butter

½ cup old-fashioned oats (use gluten-free if desired)

¼ cup raw shelled hempseed

6 ounces unsweetened coconut, for coating

INSTRUCTIONS:

1. Place the sunflower seeds, dates, walnuts, cacao powder, maple syrup, almond butter, oats, and hempseed in a large bowl. Mix well.

2. Pinch off pieces of dough and roll into twenty-four balls. Roll each ball in shredded coconut. Place in the refrigerator to harden for about 30 minutes.

Protein: 6 grams per serving (2 balls)
Active Time: 20 minutes
Refrigerator Time: 30 minutes
Total Time: 50 minutes

PEPITA AND ALMOND SQUARES

YIELD: 16 SQUARES

Almonds and pepitas are two of the highest protein–packed seeds and nuts around. Combine them with even more powerhouse ingredients and you've got a very healthy little package.

INGREDIENTS:

1   cup almonds, coarsely chopped

1   cup old-fashioned oats

⅔   cup pepitas

⅔   cup dried cranberries

½   cup unsweetened shredded coconut

¼   cup raw shelled hempseed

⅓   cup peanut butter

⅔   cup brown rice syrup

¼   cup maple syrup

2   teaspoons vanilla extract

INSTRUCTIONS:

1. Line an 8-inch square baking dish with parchment paper and come up about 3 inches on opposite sides. This will act as a handle to remove the squares from the dish.

2. In a large mixing bowl, add the almonds, oats, pepitas, cranberries, coconut, and hempseed. Mix well. Stir in the peanut butter and try to get it evenly combined. You can use your fingers when most of it is worked in.

3. Add the brown rice syrup, maple syrup, and vanilla to a small saucepan. Bring to a boil and continue boiling until it reaches the hard ball stage, 260°F, on a candy thermometer. When this temperature is reached, quickly pour over the almond mixture and stir well. It will start to harden up quickly. Pour into the prepared dish and press down firmly into the dish and as evenly as possible. Refrigerate for at least 30 minutes.

4. Grab the "handles" of the parchment paper and lift out of the dish. Place on a cutting sheet and slice into sixteen squares.

Protein: 12 grams per serving (2 squares)
Active Time: 20 minutes
Cook Time: 15 minutes
Refrigerator Time: 30 minutes
Total Time: 1 hour 5 minutes

CRUNCHY NUTS AND SEEDS PROTEIN BARS

YIELD: 16 BARS

A little miracle happens after these bars cool. They turn into a caramel-like bar that gives satisfaction to no end. Chocolaty and chewy!

INGREDIENTS:

- 2 cups chickpea flour
- 1 cup plus 2 tablespoons almond flour
- 2 tablespoons flaxseed meal
- 1 cup dairy-free milk
- 1 cup cashew butter
- ½ cup maple syrup
- ½ cup slivered almonds
- ½ cup dried cranberries
- ¼ cup sunflower seed kernels
- ½ cup dairy-free chocolate chips, melted

INSTRUCTIONS:

1. Line an 8-inch square baking dish with parchment paper and come up about 3 inches on opposite sides. This will act as a handle to remove the bars from the dish.

2. Combine the flours and flaxseed meal in a large bowl and mix well. With a heavy wooden spoon, mix in the milk, cashew butter, maple syrup, almonds, cranberries, and sunflower seeds. Lastly, mix in the melted chocolate. Add the batter to the prepared dish and press firmly into all corners and as evenly as possible. Refrigerate for at least 30 minutes.

3. Grab the "handles" of the parchment paper and lift out of the dish. Place on a cutting sheet and slice into sixteen bars.

Protein: 9 grams per serving (1 bar)
Active Time: 15 minutes
Rewfrigerator Time: 30 minutes
Total Time: 45 minutes

HIGH-PROTEIN PEANUT BUTTER COOKIE DOUGH

YIELD: 45 BALLS

Here's a simple and delicious recipe. With a few ingredients and about 15 minutes you can satisfy your sweet tooth.

INGREDIENTS:

1   cup crunchy peanut butter

1   cup maple syrup

½   teaspoon salt

1   cup chickpea flour

¾   cup almond meal flour

½   cup peanuts, chopped

½   cup cashews, chopped

½   cup old-fashioned oats

Finely ground peanuts, for coating (optional)

INSTRUCTIONS:

1. Mix the peanut butter and the syrup in a large bowl. Add the remaining ingredients and mix well. Shape into balls and eat.

2. If you'd like a little bit more of a refined look for serving, roll the balls into finely ground peanuts. For easier handling, store in the refrigerator between snacking.

Protein: 6¾ grams per serving (2 balls)
Active Time: 15 minutes
Total Time: 15 minutes

NO-BAKE CHOCOLATE PEANUT BUTTER COOKIES

YIELD: 24 COOKIES

Although these are no-bake cookies, they have the texture of baked cookies. They have no refined sugar, take 10 minutes to make, and are a favorite. That's a five-star rating!

INGREDIENTS:

½   cup unsweetened dairy-free milk

3   tablespoons dairy-free butter

⅓   cup coconut sugar

1   tablespoon unsweetened cocoa powder

⅓   cup dairy-free semi-sweet chocolate chips

1   teaspoon vanilla extract

⅓   cup creamy peanut butter

Pinch of salt

2½ cups old-fashioned oats or quick-cooking oats

¼   cup raw shelled hempseed

INSTRUCTIONS:

1. Line a baking sheet with wax paper.

2. Place the milk, butter, sugar, cocoa powder, and chocolate chips in a large saucepan. Bring to a rolling boil and then look at the timer. Let boil for 2 minutes. Stir occasionally so that the chocolate chips don't stick to the bottom of the pan before they melt. Remove from the heat and add the vanilla, peanut butter, and salt and mix until the peanut butter melts. Stir in the oats and hempseed.

3. With a spoon, drop dollops of the batter onto the prepared baking sheet. Within a minute or less you can handle them and shape into cookies. Let the cookies set for an hour or so. You can speed up the cooling and hardening process by placing them in the refrigerator.

Protein: 7 grams per serving (2 cookies)
Active Time: 5 minutes
Resting Time: 1 hour
Cook Time: 5 minutes
Total Time: 1 hour 10 minutes

APRICOT PISTACHIO ENERGY SQUARES

YIELD: 16 SQUARES

Every good flavor you can think of is in these perfect little squares. Besides heavenly apricot and dates, you have the option of drizzling chocolate over the top.

INGREDIENTS:

1½ cups pitted dates, chopped

1 cup dried apricots, chopped

1 cup cashews, chopped

½ cup old-fashioned oats

½ cup pistachios

3 tablespoons cashew butter

2 tablespoons ground ginger

⅓ cup brown rice syrup

2 tablespoons maple syrup

1 teaspoon vanilla extract

¼ cup dairy-free chocolate chips (optional)

INSTRUCTIONS:

1. Line an 8-inch square baking dish with parchment paper and come up about 3 inches on opposite sides. This will act as a handle to remove the squares from the dish.

2. Add the dates, apricots, cashews, oats, and pistachios to a large bowl. Mix in the cashew butter and ground ginger and combine as well as you can. You can use your fingers to help blend it all together.

3. In a small saucepan, add the brown rice syrup, maple syrup, and vanilla. Bring to a boil and continue boiling until it reaches the hard ball stage, 260°F, on a candy thermometer. Quickly add to the date mixture and mix well. Pour into the prepared dish and press firmly and evenly into all edges and corners. Refrigerate at least 30 minutes.

4. Grab the "handles" of the parchment paper and lift out of the dish. Place on a cutting sheet and slice into sixteen squares.

5. If desired, melt the chocolate chips in a microwave or in a small saucepan. Drizzle back and forth over the bars.

Protein: 8 grams per serving (2 squares)
Active Time: 15 minutes
Cook Time: 10 minutes
Refrigerator Time: 30 minutes
Total Time: 55 minutes

CARROT CAKE TWO-BITE BALLS

YIELD: 16 BALLS

Carrot cake! I kid you not. Everything for a carrot cake is in here, all rolled up into perfect little balls. You can roll some in coconut and leave others plain. They are so pretty.

INGREDIENTS:

1 cup old-fashioned oats

½ cup almond meal

½ cup pecans

⅓ cup plus 2 tablespoons unsweetened shredded coconut, divided

3 medium carrots, grated

15 dates, pitted

2 tablespoons unsweetened cocoa powder

2 tablespoons almond butter

1 teaspoon ground cinnamon

½ teaspoon ground nutmeg

½ teaspoon ground ginger

INSTRUCTIONS:

1. Add the oats, almond meal, pecans, ⅓ cup coconut, carrots, dates, and cocoa powder to a food processor. Mix on high until well processed. You may have to scrape down the edges a couple of times to make sure the dates aren't clumping. Add the almond butter, cinnamon, nutmeg, and ginger. Mix again until well mixed. Scrape down again if needed.

2. Transfer to a flat surface and make sure all is blended well. Use your hands if necessary. Pinch off pieces of dough and roll into sixteen balls. Roll the balls in additional shredded coconut, if desired.

Protein: 8 grams per serving (2 balls)
Active Time: 20 minutes
Total Time: 20 minutes

CHOCOLATE TRAIL MIX BARS

YIELD: 8 BARS

These big and sturdy bars are great for the trail or even for just sitting in the backyard. Melted chocolate is included, so they are nice and chocolaty, too.

INGREDIENTS:

¾ cup old-fashioned oats

½ cup bran flakes cereal

½ cup mixed nuts, chopped

¼ cup dried cherries

¼ cup dried cranberries

¼ cup raw shelled hempseed

3 tablespoons peanut butter

¼ cup maple syrup

½ cup dairy-free chocolate chips, melted

INSTRUCTIONS:

1. Line an 8-inch square baking dish with parchment paper and come up about 3 inches on opposite sides. This will act as a handle to remove the bars from the dish.

2. Add the oats, cereal, nuts, cherries, cranberries, and hempseed to a large bowl and mix well.

3. Mix the peanut butter and syrup together and pour into the large bowl. Mix well. Add the melted chocolate and mix again.

4. Press firmly into the prepared dish and into all corners. Let set in the refrigerator for 30 minutes.

5. Grab the "handles" of the parchment paper and lift out of the dish. Place on a cutting board and slice down the center. Turn and make three even cuts, which will give you eight long bars.

Protein: 16 grams per serving (1 bar)
Active Time: 20 minutes
Refrigerator Time: 30 minutes
Total Time: 50 minutes

The High-Protein Vegan Cookbook

VANILLA ALMOND DATE BALLS

YIELD: 20 BALLS

Vanilla is such a great flavor, and it seems to make something a treat without going over the top. Almond flour and protein powder is added for an extra oomph of protein.

INGREDIENTS:

1½ cups almond flour

16 dates, pitted

4   tablespoons sunflower seed kernels

4   tablespoons vanilla protein powder

2   tablespoons flaxseed meal

1   teaspoon vanilla extract

Pinch of salt

2   tablespoons sunflower seed kernels, ground fine in a small food processor

INSTRUCTIONS:

Place all the ingredients except the ground sunflower seeds in a food processor. Process on high until all is combined well and forms a ball. Transfer into a large bowl and form twenty balls. This dough works well by squeezing each one a few times to form a ball. Roll in ground sunflower seeds.

Protein: 8 grams per serving (2 balls)
Active Time: 20 minutes
Total Time: 20 minutes

LAYERED OAT AND CHOCOLATE BARS

YIELD: 16 SQUARES

You wouldn't think that no-bake bars could look like this and hold together like this, but they do. They're more like a candy bar than anything else, except they're loaded with protein.

INGREDIENTS:

1 cup dairy-free butter

½ cup coconut sugar

1 teaspoon vanilla extract

3 cups quick-cooking oats

¼ cup raw shelled hempseed

2 tablespoons protein powder

1 cup dairy-free chocolate chips

½ cup peanut butter

INSTRUCTIONS:

1. Line an 8-inch square baking dish with parchment paper and come up about 3 inches on opposite sides. This will act as a handle to remove the squares from the dish.

2. In a medium saucepan, melt the butter over medium-high heat. Add the sugar and vanilla. Mix the in oats and cook for 2 minutes. Add the hempseed and protein powder and mix well. Transfer half of the mixture into the prepared dish and press firmly and evenly into all edges and corners.

3. Place the chocolate and peanut butter in a small saucepan. Heat over low heat until chocolate is melted and all is well combined. Pour over the bottom layer in the prepared dish and smooth evenly all over the top. Crumble the remaining oat mixture over the top as evenly as possible and lightly press into the chocolate.

4. Refrigerate for at least 1 hour.

5. Grab the "handles" of the parchment paper and lift out of the dish. Place on a cutting sheet and slice into sixteen squares.

Protein: 7 grams per serving (1 square)
Active Time: 20 minutes
Cook Time: 5 minutes
Refrigerator time: 1 hour
Total Time: 1 hour 25 minutes

The High-Protein Vegan Cookbook

PUMP UP THE POWER ENERGY BALLS

YIELD: 32 BALLS

No-bake treats are so easy to make. Currants are readily available, and they seem to have been made to be combined with pepitas . . . and hempseed . . . and peanut butter . . .

INGREDIENTS:

1   cup old-fashioned oats

¾   cup almond meal

⅓   cup wheat germ

¼   cup flaxseed meal

¼   cup pepitas

2   tablespoons raw shelled hempseed

1   teaspoon ground cinnamon

¼   teaspoon ground nutmeg

½   cup dried currants

½   cup peanut butter

⅓   cup maple syrup

1   teaspoon vanilla extract

¼   teaspoon salt

INSTRUCTIONS:

1. Mix the oats, almond meal, wheat germ, flaxseed meal, pepitas, hempseed, cinnamon, nutmeg, and currants together in a medium bowl.

2. Add the peanut butter, maple syrup, vanilla, and salt to the bowl of a stand mixer. Mix on medium speed until well combined. Pour the dry ingredients into the wet mixture. Mix on low until well combined.

3. Roll into thirty-two balls.

Protein: 10 grams per serving (3 balls)
Active Time: 20 minutes
Total Time: 20 minutes

CHAPTER FIVE

PROTEIN-PACKED DINNERS

AIR-FRIED STICKY RICE FEATURING SEITAN

YIELD: 4 SERVINGS

This dinner recipe will knock your socks off. The sweet and spicy sauce is fast and easy to make. There's a skillet option, too!

INGREDIENTS:

2   cups jasmine rice

½   cup soy sauce or gluten-free tamari

4   tablespoons maple syrup

4   cloves garlic, finely chopped

2   teaspoons Chinese five spice

½   teaspoon ground ginger

4   tablespoons white wine or rice vinegar

1   pound cremini mushrooms, wiped clean, or any large mushrooms cut in half

1   cup Pressure Cooker Thai Nuggets (page 288)

½   cup frozen peas

INSTRUCTIONS:

1. Add the rice to a large saucepan with 2 cups water. Cover and bring to a boil. Turn the heat down to medium and cook for about 20 minutes or until the water is absorbed.

2. If your air fryer doesn't have a built-in insert, then insert one now.

3. Mix the soy sauce, maple syrup, garlic, Chinese five spice, ginger, and white wine together in a small bowl and set aside.

4. Place the mushrooms in the air fryer. If you can set your temperature, set it to 350°F. Otherwise, just turn it on—my air fryer temperature is built in and always cooks at 338°F. Cook for 10 minutes. Open the air fryer and add the seitan nuggets. If you don't have a built-in self-stirrer in your air fryer, then stir. Pour the liquid mixture and peas over the top. Stir and cook 5 minutes.

5. Add rice and stir well. Heat for 2 minutes. Serve.

Note: If you don't have an air fryer, you can make this dish in a skillet. Precook the jasmine rice and set aside. Mix together the next six ingredients and set aside. Heat a tablespoon of oil in a large skillet. Add mushrooms and cook 10 minutes over medium-high heat. Pour the liquid mixture over the mushrooms. Add peas and seitan nuggets and cook for 5 more minutes. Add the cooked rice, stir well, and heat through.

Protein: 20 grams per serving
Active Time: 30 minutes
Cook Time: 30 minutes
Total Time: 1 hour

YIELD: 4 SERVINGS

There's nothing like a casserole baking in the oven, and this one smells so good. With two different sauces, along with the veggies and tortillas, this dinner is a quadruple win.

INGREDIENTS:

Filling

1 cup diced yellow bell pepper

1 sweet potato, peeled and chopped into bite-size pieces

1 cup diced white onion

1 tablespoon extra virgin olive oil

1 teaspoon salt, divided

¼ teaspoon ground black pepper

1 15-ounce can black beans, drained and rinsed

2 ounces tempeh, pulsed fine

1 teaspoon ground cumin

1 teaspoon chili powder

2 cloves garlic, minced

2 cups store-bought red enchilada sauce

6 small corn tortillas

White Sauce

2 tablespoons dairy-free butter

3 tablespoons flour

1½ cups dairy-free milk

1 tablespoon nutritional yeast

Protein: 14 grams per serving
Active Time: 30 minutes
Cook Time: 1 hour
Total Time: 1 hour 30 minutes

INSTRUCTIONS:

Filling

1. Preheat the oven to 400°F.

2. Place the bell pepper, sweet potato, and onion on a baking sheet. Sprinkle with the oil and toss to make sure all the vegetables are coated. Spread out on the baking sheet and season with ½ teaspoon salt and pepper. Place in the oven and roast for 15 minutes. Remove from the oven, stir, and return to the oven for another 15 minutes. Check to see if sweet potatoes can be easily pierced with a fork. If not, stir and cook for up to another 10 minutes. Remove from the oven and set aside. Lower the oven temperature to 350°F.

3. Add the roasted vegetables, beans, tempeh, cumin, chili powder, and garlic to a medium bowl.

4. Spread ¼ cup enchilada sauce in the bottom of an 8-inch square glass casserole dish.

5. Cut four tortillas into fourths. Lay four of the quarters in each corner of the casserole with the V toward the corner. Lay one whole tortilla right in the center. Top with a third of the vegetable mixture and spread evenly over the tortillas. Drizzle another ¼ cup of the enchilada sauce. Lay another layer of tortillas as you did before. Top with another layer using a third of the vegetable mixture and drizzle on another ¼ cup enchilada sauce. Lay another layer of tortillas and then the

remainder of the vegetable mixture. Keep the remaining enchilada sauce aside.

White Sauce

6. Melt the butter in a medium saucepan. Stir in the flour and cook for 1 minute. Add the milk and heat over medium-high heat to a low boil. Add the nutritional yeast and continue to cook and stir until the sauce thickens and cooks down by about ¼ cup. Remove from the heat.

Assembly

7. Pour the remaining enchilada sauce over the top of the casserole and spread evenly. Drizzle the white sauce back and forth over the top but do not spread. Cover with either the lid to the casserole dish or a sheet of aluminum foil. Bake for 30 minutes.

8. Take the enchilada casserole out of the oven and also remove the foil. Let sit for 10 minutes before serving in squares.

KALE WHITE BEAN SOUP

YIELD: 6 SERVINGS

This is an easy and delicious recipe that serves up a complete meal. It's great for any night of the week. Presoak the beans overnight and you're on your way.

INGREDIENTS:

1   pound navy beans

1   tablespoon coconut oil

½   cup coarsely chopped onions

1   clove garlic, minced

¼   cup nutritional yeast

1   red bell pepper, diced

4   Roma tomatoes, chopped

2   cups sliced carrots

5   cups vegetable broth

1   teaspoon Italian seasoning

2   teaspoons salt

½   teaspoon ground black pepper

1   pound kale, de-stemmed and coarsely chopped

INSTRUCTIONS:

1. Place the beans in a large stockpot and cover with water by about 3 inches. Let it sit overnight to let the beans expand. If you want to do the quick method for preparing the beans—instead of soaking overnight—then cover beans with water by 2 inches in the stockpot. Cover with a lid and bring to a boil. Remove from the heat and let stand, uncovered, 1 hour. Drain beans in a colander and set aside.

2. Put the oil in the same stockpot and heat over medium heat. Add the onions and sauté for about 10 to 15 minutes until soft and translucent. Add the garlic and cook, stirring, for 1 minute. Add 4 cups water, the beans, nutritional yeast, bell pepper, tomatoes, carrots, broth, Italian seasoning, salt, and pepper. Cover and bring to a boil. Uncover and turn down to a simmer. Cook until beans are tender, about 1 to 1½ hours.

3. Stir in kale and 2 cups water and simmer, uncovered, until kale is tender, about 12 to 15 minutes.

Protein: 14 grams per serving
Overnight Time: 8 hours
Active Time: 20 minutes
Cook Time: 2 hours
Total Time: 10 hours 20 minutes

SLOW COOKER SEITAN BOURGUIGNON

YIELD: 4 SERVINGS

This dinner dish is rich in taste with mushrooms, carrots, and seitan. It's so simple to make, and you'll be amazed at its depth of flavors.

INGREDIENTS:

2   tablespoons extra virgin olive oil

1   cup diced yellow onion

1½ cups sliced carrots

2   tablespoons dairy-free butter, divided

2   cloves garlic, minced

2   tablespoons flour

2½ cups vegetable broth

1   tablespoon liquid smoke

2   tablespoons tomato paste

1   cup good Burgundy wine

1   bay leaf

½   teaspoon thyme

1   teaspoon salt

1   pound mushrooms, sliced

2   cups Slow Cooker Versatile Seitan Balls, cubed (page 279)

INSTRUCTIONS:

1. Heat the oil in a large skillet. Add the onion and carrots and sauté about 10 to 15 minutes or until the onions are translucent. Add 1 tablespoon butter. Add the garlic and cook for another minute.

2. Add the flour and stir to coat everything and cook for another minute. Make sure the flour has been worked all the way in and the mixture does not show any dry flour.

3. Add all the ingredients from the skillet to the slow cooker. Stir in ½ cup water, the broth, liquid smoke, tomato paste, wine, bay leaf, thyme, and salt. Cook on low for 6 to 8 hours.

4. About an hour before serving, sauté the mushrooms in a tablespoon of butter in a large skillet for about 10 minutes. Add the mushrooms and seitan to the slow cooker and cook another hour.

5. Serve by itself or with noodles, potatoes, or rice.

Protein: 34 grams per serving
Active Time: 30 minutes
Cook Time: 9 hours
Total Time: 9 hours 30 minutes

THREE-LAYER TACOS WITH KALE SLAW

YIELD: 3 SERVINGS

You'll want taco night every night of the week with these overflowing tacos. The tofu gets marinated with the pinto beans, and a spicy-sweet slaw serves as a topping.

INGREDIENTS:

Filling

1   tablespoon taco seasoning

3   tablespoons tamari

8   ounces extra-firm tofu, drained, pressed (page 17), and cut into ½-inch chunks

1   15-ounce can pinto beans, drained and rinsed

¼   cup finely diced white onion

2   Roma tomatoes, finely diced

½   teaspoon salt

Pinch of ground black pepper

1   teaspoon chopped parsley

Kale Slaw

1   cup de-stemmed and coarsely chopped kale

1   tablespoon lemon juice

1   cup thinly sliced purple cabbage

1   cup thinly sliced green cabbage

¼   cup shredded carrots

2   tablespoons dairy-free mayonnaise

1   tablespoon lime juice

1   teaspoon maple syrup

1   chipotle pepper in adobo sauce, chopped finely

To Assemble

6   taco shells

INSTRUCTIONS:

Filling

1. Mix the taco seasoning and tamari in a small bowl. Set aside.

2. Add the tofu to the tamari mix and toss. Marinate while working on the bean mixture and slaw.

3. Add the beans, onion, tomatoes, salt, pepper, and parsley to a small bowl. Toss and set aside to meld.

Kale Slaw

4. Add the kale to a medium bowl and add the lemon juice. Massage the kale with your hands to soften it up. Add both cabbages, the carrots, mayonnaise, lime juice, maple syrup, and chili in adobo sauce. Mix well.

Assembly

5. Assemble the tacos by layering the shells with the bean mixture, tofu, and finally the slaw.

Protein: 30 grams per serving (2 tacos)
Active Time: 25 minutes
Total Time: 25 minutes

TEMPEH TACOS WITH BREADED AND BAKED CAULIFLOWER

YIELD: 4 SERVINGS

Now's the time for all good cooks to bake breaded cauliflower. There are so many layers of flavor that you could easily want to have two.

INGREDIENTS:

- 8 ounces original tempeh
- 3 tablespoons hot sauce (such as Frank's), divided
- ¼ cup plus 2 tablespoons unsweetened dairy-free milk, divided
- 1 small head cauliflower
- 1 cup whole wheat flour
- 2 tablespoons taco seasoning
- ½ cup panko breadcrumbs
- 2 tablespoons nutritional yeast
- 1 tablespoon coconut oil
- 2 cups shredded romaine lettuce
- 8 taco shells
- 2 Roma tomatoes, chopped
- Lime wedges (optional)
- Salsa (optional)

Protein: 30 grams per serving (2 tacos)
Active Time: 15 minutes
Marinating Time: 1 hour
Cook Time: 30 minutes
Total Time: 1 hour 45 minutes

INSTRUCTIONS:

1. Preheat the oven to 350°F.

2. Cut the tempeh widthwise into ¼-inch strips, then tear those into about ½-inch pieces.

3. Mix 1 tablespoon hot sauce and 2 tablespoons milk together in a small bowl. Add tempeh and toss. Let marinate for 1 hour.

4. Meanwhile, prepare the cauliflower by cutting the florets into small bite-size pieces.

5. Mix 2 tablespoons of hot sauce and ¼ cup milk in a large bowl. Add the cauliflower and toss.

6. Add the flour, taco seasoning, panko, and nutritional yeast to a large bowl and mix well.

7. Take the cauliflower out of the wet mixture and add to the flour mixture and toss to coat all of the florets. Place on a baking sheet and bake for 20 to 30 minutes, turning after 15 minutes. You will be able to pierce them easily with a fork when done.

8. While the cauliflower is baking, heat the oil in a small skillet over medium-high heat and add the tempeh. Cook for about 2 minutes, flipping occasionally, until the pieces become golden brown. Remove from the heat to a paper towel.

9. Assemble the taco by laying some lettuce in the bottom of a shell and spooning in some tempeh, cauliflower, and tomato. Serve with lime wedges and salsa, if desired.

The High-Protein Vegan Cookbook

SLOW COOKER CHIPOTLE TACOS

YIELD: 4 SERVINGS

The slow cooker has never made life so easy. Here's an unusual list of ingredients that sends these tacos off the chart. You would never guess what's included.

INGREDIENTS:

2 15-ounce cans pinto beans, drained and rinsed

1 cup corn, fresh, frozen, or canned

3 ounces chipotle pepper in adobo sauce (about 2 peppers), chopped

6 ounces tomato paste

¾ cup Thai sweet chili sauce

1 tablespoon unsweetened cocoa powder

1½ teaspoons taco seasoning

8 white corn taco shells or tortillas, or your favorite

Favorite toppings: spinach, lettuce, black olives, lime, avocado, peppers

INSTRUCTIONS:

1. Put everything in the crockpot except the taco shells and toppings. Cook on low for 3 to 4 hours or on high for 1½ to 2 hours.

2. Spread quite a bit of the filling on your taco shells, hard or soft. Add your favorite toppings.

Protein: 20 grams per serving (2 tacos)
Active Time: 15 minutes
Cook Time: 4 hours
Total Time: 4 hours 15 minutes

BROCCOLI TOFU QUICHE

YIELD: 6 SERVINGS

Elegance and protein are wrapped up in this pretty quiche. It's full of veggies and is a special dinner that reheats perfectly. You can bake this quiche in a springform pan or a pie plate.

INGREDIENTS:

Cashew Cheese

¼ cup raw cashews, soaked for 1 hour

½ cup water

1 tablespoon nutritional yeast

2 tablespoons tapioca flour

1 tablespoon red miso

½ teaspoon cider vinegar

¼ teaspoon salt

¼ teaspoon garlic powder

Quiche

1 tablespoon extra virgin olive oil

1 cup baby spinach

½ cup diced red onion

1 cup diced red bell pepper (about one small pepper)

8 ounces cremini mushrooms, sliced

1½ cups broccoli, inner stalks cut into cubes and florets cut into bites

3 cloves garlic, chopped fine

1 cup canned black beans, drained and rinsed

16 ounces extra-firm tofu, drained and pressed (page 17)

¼ cup dairy-free milk

¼ teaspoon turmeric

2 teaspoons oregano

1 teaspoon salt

¼ teaspoon ground black pepper

1 package vegan piecrust with 2 crusts

INSTRUCTIONS:

Cashew Cheese

1. Add all the cheese ingredients to a blender. Blend until smooth.

2. Pour into a small saucepan and cook over medium-high heat, stirring most of the time. It will thicken and become a bit stretchy within 5 minutes. If it seems too thick to combine with the quiche ingredients, then you can add a drop of water at a time. Set aside.

Quiche

3. Preheat the oven to 350°F.

4. Heat the oil in a large skillet over medium heat. Add the baby spinach and cook until it is wilted. Remove from the pan and set aside. Add the onion, bell pepper, mushrooms, and broccoli to the skillet and sauté for about 10 to 15 minutes until the onion is translucent. Add the garlic and cook 2 more minutes. Stir in the black beans and heat through. Pour into a large mixing bowl.

5. Break the tofu into a blender and add the milk, cashew cheese, turmeric, oregano, salt, and pepper. Blend as smooth as possible. Add the

blended mixture to the sautéed vegetables and mix well.

6. Pour into one piecrust. Cover with the second piecrust and crimp the edge. If you use a springform pan, make a rolled edge in the bottom crust and lay the top crust over the top of the ingredients. Bake the quiche for 30 minutes.

Protein: 21 grams protein per serving
Active Time: 30 minutes
Soaking Time: 1 hour
Cook Time: 50 minutes
Total Time: 2 hours 20 minutes

PANANG SEITAN CURRY

YIELD: 6 SERVINGS

Peanut sauce, red curry paste, and a little hot sauce are all added to make sweet and spicy a major component of this seitan and vegetable feast.

INGREDIENTS:

1 cup red quinoa

1 sweet potato, peeled and chopped into bite-size pieces

1 tablespoon extra virgin olive oil

1 red bell pepper, diced

¼ cup finely chopped shallot

2 cloves garlic, finely diced

¼ cup creamy peanut butter

2 tablespoons red curry paste

1 teaspoon sriracha

2 teaspoons turmeric

1 teaspoon ground ginger

1 teaspoon ground cumin

1 14-ounce can coconut cream

1 tablespoon lime juice

½ teaspoon salt

2 cups Pressure Cooker Thai Nuggets (page 288)

INSTRUCTIONS:

1. Place the quinoa in a sieve and rinse well. Place the quinoa in a medium saucepan and cover with 2 cups water. Bring to a boil and then turn the heat down and cover. Simmer for about 15 to 20 minutes or until all the water is absorbed and quinoa is tender. Set aside, covered.

2. Add water to a medium saucepan with a steamer insert and bring to a boil. Add sweet potato to the insert and steam over boiling water for 10 minutes.

3. Heat the oil in a large skillet over medium heat. Add the bell pepper and sauté for 10 minutes. Add the shallots and garlic and cook for 2 minutes. Stir in the peanut butter, red curry paste, sriracha, turmeric, ginger, and cumin. Cook for 5 minutes, stirring occasionally. Stir in 1 cup water, the coconut cream, lime juice, and salt. Add the sweet potato and seitan nuggets. Stir and turn heat to medium high. Bring to a low boil, turn down the heat to a simmer, and cover. Cook for 10 to 15 minutes.

4. Serve with quinoa.

Protein: 26 grams protein per serving
Active Time: 20 minutes
Cook Time: 45 minutes
Total Time: 1 hour 5 minutes

POLENTA WITH RICH MUSHROOM GRAVY

YIELD: 4 SERVINGS

Polenta is a wonder, and it's so easy to make. Top it with protein-rich mushroom gravy for a meal that you'll be really glad you tried.

INGREDIENTS:

Polenta

¼ cup coconut oil

1 tablespoon chopped shallot

3 cloves garlic, minced

1 teaspoon dried basil

½ cup dry white wine, such as chardonnay

3 cups vegetable broth

⅓ cup chopped Roma tomatoes

½ teaspoon salt

1 cup cornmeal

Mushroom Gravy

2 tablespoons extra virgin olive oil

1 pound button mushrooms, sliced

1 tablespoon chopped shallots

1 clove garlic, finely chopped

3 tablespoons flour

2 cups vegetable broth

½ teaspoon salt

¼ teaspoon ground black pepper

1 cup Pressure Cooker Tender Patties, crumbled (page 286)

_____

Protein: 22 grams per serving
Active Time: 20 minutes
Cook Time: 45 minutes
Total Time: 1 hour 5 minutes

INSTRUCTIONS:

Polenta

1. Grease a 9-inch square pan.

2. Heat the coconut oil in a large saucepan over medium-high heat. Add the shallot and cook for 3 to 5 minutes or until tender. Add the garlic and basil and cook for another minute. Stir in the wine and bring to a boil. Reduce the heat and simmer for 5 minutes. Add the broth, tomatoes, and salt. Bring to a boil and then reduce the heat and add the cornmeal. Cook and stir for 15 to 20 minutes or until the polenta is thickened and pulls away from the side of the pan.

3. Pour into the prepared pan and spread evenly out to all 4 corners. Set aside to cool to room temperature. This should take about 20 to 30 minutes.

Mushroom Gravy

4. While the polenta is cooling, make the mushroom gravy: Heat the olive oil in a skillet. Add mushrooms and sauté 10 to 15 minutes. Add the shallots and sauté for 3 to 5 minutes. Stir in the garlic and flour and cook for 1 more minute. Add the vegetable broth, salt, and pepper. Bring to a boil and then turn down to medium and cook about 5 minutes or until it has thickened a bit. Add the crumbled patties and cook for 5 more minutes to heat through.

5. Slice the polenta into squares and serve a slice or two on a plate with mushroom gravy ladled on top.

ARTICHOKE FLATBREAD WITH CRUMBLED SEITAN

YIELD: 2 SERVINGS

You have to make this! Flatbread topped with these simple ingredients adds up to so much pleasure and protein.

INGREDIENTS:

Cashew Cheese

¾ cup raw cashews, soaked from 1 hour to overnight and drained

½ cup water

1 tablespoon nutritional yeast

1 tablespoon tapioca starch or tapioca flour

½ teaspoon garlic powder

½ teaspoon onion powder

1 tablespoon lemon juice

To Assemble

2 8-inch flatbreads

¼ cup baby spinach, cut in strips

½ cup Steamed Seitan Smoky Nuggets (page 283)

14 ounces artichoke hearts in water, discarded

1 Roma tomato, chopped

¼ cup canned sliced black olives

Raw shelled hempseed, for topping

INSTRUCTIONS:

Cashew Cheese

1. Add all of the cheese ingredients to a blender and blend until smooth. Turn this blended mixture into a saucepan. Cook over medium heat and stir until the sauce thickens a bit. It will take 5 to 10 minutes. Take off the heat to cool.

Assembly

2. Spread a ½-cup layer of cashew cheese on each flatbread. Sprinkle half of the spinach on each flatbread. Divide the seitan, artichokes, tomatoes, and olives and sprinkle evenly over each flatbread.

3. Serve with hempseed to sprinkle over top.

Protein: 39 grams per serving
Active Time: 20 minutes
Soaking Time: 1 hour
Cook Time: 10 minutes
Total Time: 1 hour 30 minutes

VEGETABLE JUMBLE WITH THAI SEITAN

YIELD: 6 SERVINGS

Here's an eclectic mix of all the best and most popular vegetables. A tasty seitan is added, and all of the spices make this jumble pop with flavor.

INGREDIENTS:

2   carrots, sliced thinly

1   small head cauliflower, cut into florets

1   small head broccoli, cut into florets

1   tablespoon extra virgin olive oil

1   small white onion, diced

1   red bell pepper, julienned

8   ounces mushrooms, sliced

1   cup Pressure Cooker Thai Nuggets (page 288)

¼   teaspoon thyme

¼   teaspoon basil

½   teaspoon salt

¼   teaspoon ground black pepper

INSTRUCTIONS:

1. Add water to a medium saucepan with a steamer insert and bring to a boil. Add the carrots and cauliflower to the insert and steam over boiling water for 5 minutes.

2. Add the broccoli on top of the cauliflower and steam for 10 more minutes. Poke all the vegetables and make sure they can be easily pierced with a fork. Do not overcook. Al dente is best.

3. Heat the oil in a large skillet. Add the onion and bell pepper and sauté for 10 minutes. Add the mushrooms to the skillet and cook for 10 more minutes. Add the seitan nuggets and all of the herbs and spices. Stir and heat through for about 2 minutes. Add the cauliflower mixture, stir well, and cook another 5 minutes.

Protein: 19 grams per serving
Active Time: 15 minutes
Cook Time: 30 minutes
Total Time: 45 minutes

SUPERPOWER STUFFED POBLANO PEPPERS

YIELD: 4 SERVINGS

Four huge roasted peppers are stuffed with veggies and spices. Line them up in a casserole for a Southwestern-style meal you won't soon forget. You can soak the cashews the night before so you can dive right in to the preparation.

INGREDIENTS:

Peppers and Stuffing

4   poblano peppers

¾   cup quinoa

1½ cups vegetable broth

1   tablespoon coconut oil

½   cup diced white onion

1   clove garlic, minced

1   cup cooked black beans, drained and rinsed

½   cup corn, fresh, frozen or canned

1   chipotle pepper in adobo sauce, chopped small, and 1 tablespoon adobo sauce

1   teaspoon chili powder

½   teaspoon ground cumin

½   teaspoon salt

Cashew Cheese Sauce

¾   cup raw cashews, soaked from 1 hour to overnight and drained

2   tablespoons nutritional yeast

1   tablespoon tapioca starch (also called tapioca flour)

½   teaspoon garlic powder

½   teaspoon onion powder

1   tablespoon lemon juice

INSTRUCTIONS:

Peppers and Stuffing

1. Heat the broiler.

2. Place the peppers on a baking sheet and set on the top shelf of the broiler. Turn often with tongs to get all sides blackened. Let the peppers cool and then rub off the blackened skin with a damp paper towel or peel with a paring knife. Just grab an edge of the skin with the knife and peel off. Be careful not to tear up the peppers, since they will be stuffed. They will probably split naturally at one spot so use that as your opening to remove the seeds. Set aside.

3. Rinse the quinoa and place in a large saucepan. Pour in the vegetable broth and bring to a boil. Cover and turn down heat to medium and cook for about 15 minutes or until all the liquid is absorbed. Remove from the heat and set aside with the cover on.

4. Heat the oil in a small skillet over medium heat. Add the onion and cook 10 to 15 minutes or until translucent. Stir in the garlic and cook for 1 more minute.

5. Heat the oven to 350°F.

6. Add the quinoa, beans, corn, chili pepper, extra adobo sauce, chili powder, cumin, and salt to a large bowl. Mix well. Stuff each pepper with ¼ of the stuffing and place in a casserole that will hold them snugly. Bake for 15 to 20 minutes.

The High-Protein Vegan Cookbook

Cashew Cheese Sauce

7. Add all the ingredients to a blender and blend until smooth. Turn this blended mixture into a saucepan. Cook on medium heat and stir until the sauce thickens a bit. It will take about 5 to 10 minutes.

Assembly

8. Remove the stuffed peppers from the oven and drizzle cheese sauce over everything.

Protein: 17 grams per serving
Active Time: 15 minutes
Soaking Time: 1 hour
Cook Time: 45 minutes
Total Time: 2 hours

ARROZ CON SEITAN

YIELD: 4 SERVINGS

Skillet cooking has never been easier. Jasmine rice is added to a pan of veggies and all is cooked together for a filling protein win.

INGREDIENTS:

- 2 tablespoons extra virgin olive oil
- 1 cup chopped onion
- 1 bell pepper, chopped
- 1 clove garlic, minced
- 2 cups jasmine rice
- 1 15-ounce can tomatoes, diced
- 1 cup vegetable broth
- 2 cups Steamed Seitan Chipotle Links, torn into bite-size pieces (page 284)
- 8 ounces peas, fresh, frozen, or canned (optional)
- 1 teaspoon salt
- ¼ teaspoon ground black pepper

INSTRUCTIONS:

1. Add the oil to a large skillet that has a cover and heat over medium-high heat. Add the onions and bell peppers and sauté for 10 minutes. Add the garlic and stir to heat through. Add the rice, tomatoes, and vegetable broth. Stir and pat down with the back of a wooden spoon to make sure all the rice is in liquid. Cover, raise to a boil, and turn down immediately to simmer for 15 minutes. Check to see if rice is done and most of the liquid is cooked away.

2. Lightly stir in the seitan, peas (if using) salt, and pepper, and replace the cover. Let steam for 10 minutes on low heat.

Protein: 34 grams per serving
Active Time: 20 minutes
Cook Time: 35 minutes
Total Time: 55 minutes

CHICKPEA TORTILLA FAJITA STACK

YIELD: 4 SERVINGS

Chickpea flour tortillas have a crepe-like texture and feature just the right savory blend. Stacked with layers of spicy beans and mushrooms, these fajitas are fantastic. Who doesn't like Mexican-style food?

INGREDIENTS:

Chickpea Tortillas

1 tablespoon ground chia seeds

1 cup chickpea flour

¼ teaspoon sea salt

½ teaspoon ground cumin

2 tablespoons extra virgin olive oil

Filling

1 tablespoon extra virgin olive oil

½ cup diced white onion

1 yellow bell pepper, diced

8 ounces white mushrooms, diced

½ cup diced tomatoes

2 teaspoons fajita seasoning

½ teaspoon salt

¼ teaspoon ground black pepper

1 15-ounce can pinto beans, drained and rinsed

2 tablespoons raw shelled hempseed

Salsa, for garnish

Avocado, for garnish

INSTRUCTIONS:

Chickpea Tortillas

1. Mix ground chia seeds with 3 tablespoons water. Set aside.

2. Add 1 cup water, the chickpea flour, chia seed mixture, salt, and cumin to a medium bowl.

3. Mix until just combined.

4. Add 2 tablespoons oil to an 8-inch skillet and heat to medium high.

5. Add ¼ cup chickpea batter and tilt the pan in a circular tilt to let the batter flow to cover the bottom of the pan, as you would a crepe.

6. Cook until golden brown and flip. Cook for another minute and remove to a plate. Continue until all the batter is gone and the tortillas are made.

Filling

7. Add the oil to a large skillet and heat to medium high. Add the onion, bell pepper, and mushrooms and sauté 10 to 15 minutes or until the onion is translucent. Add the tomatoes, fajita seasoning, salt, and pepper and cook for 5 minutes. Add the beans and hempseed. Heat through.

Protein: 17 grams per serving
Active Time: 20 minutes
Total Time: 20 minutes

Assembly

8. Layer the chickpea tortilla stack starting with one tortilla on a plate. Spoon on about ½ cup filling. Add another tortilla and ½ cup filling and continue until the filling is all gone. Top with a tortilla, salsa, and avocado. Cut into quarters in a pie shape and serve.

SEITAN BALLS WITH SLOW COOKER SPAGHETTI SAUCE

YIELD: 6 SERVINGS

This is one of those recipes that the slow cooker was made for. The sauce is best when cooked low and slow.

INGREDIENTS:

2 tablespoons extra virgin olive oil

2 cups finely diced yellow onion

4 cloves garlic, finely diced

2 28-ounce cans diced tomatoes

4 6-ounce cans tomato paste

1 teaspoon crumbled bay leaf

2 tablespoons coconut sugar

1 teaspoon oregano

1 teaspoon basil

1 teaspoon salt

½ teaspoon ground black pepper

1½ cups Slow Cooker Versatile Seitan Balls (page 279)

12 ounces spaghetti

INSTRUCTIONS:

1. Add the oil to a large skillet and heat to medium high. Add the onion and sauté until it is translucent, about 10 to 15 minutes. Turn down the heat to medium and add garlic and cook for 2 more minutes. Add all the ingredients (except the seitan and pasta) to the slow cooker, plus 1½ cups water. Cook on low for 6 to 8 hours, adding the seitan in the last hour. If you want to cook on high, then cook 3 to 4 hours adding the seitan for the last half hour.

2. Cook the spaghetti according to package directions and serve with seitan pasta sauce.

Protein: 27 grams per serving
Active Time: 15 minutes
Cook Time: 8 hours
Total Time: 8 hours 15 minutes

BAKED TOFU WITH SPICY TAHINI SAUCE

YIELD: 4 SERVINGS

There's no need for takeout when you're armed with this recipe. Baked tofu is dredged in a spicy sauce that can be whipped up in an instant. You might be tempted to double the topping.

INGREDIENTS:

1½ cups jasmine rice

14 ounces extra-firm tofu, drained, pressed (page 17), and cut into ½-inch cubes

1¼ cups tahini

¼ cup tamari

¼ cup rice vinegar

¼ cup maple syrup

½ teaspoon ground ginger

1 clove garlic, minced

½ teaspoon sriracha

Fresh thyme, for garnish (optional)

INSTRUCTIONS:

1. Preheat the oven to 400°F. Line a baking sheet with parchment paper.

2. Add the rice to a saucepan and cover with 3 cups water. Cover, bring to a boil, and turn down heat. Cook covered for about 15 minutes or until water is absorbed.

3. Place the tofu cubes on the prepared baking sheet and bake for 15 minutes. Flip with a spatula and cook for 10 more minutes. Set aside.

4. While the tofu is baking, make the sauce: Add tahini, tamari, ½ cup water, rice vinegar, maple syrup, ginger, garlic, and sriracha to a saucepan. Mix well and heat through until hot and creamy.

5. Toss in prepared tofu and serve hot over rice. Garnish with the thyme, if desired.

Protein: 20 grams per serving
Active Time: 15 minutes
Cook Time: 25 minutes
Total Time: 40 minutes

STUFFED SWEET POTATOES WITH TAHINI DRESSING

YIELD: 2 SERVINGS

This recipe makes a complete meal in one pretty package. Sweet and savory flavors are served together, and then slathered with the perfect dressing as a foil.

INGREDIENTS:

Sweet Potatoes and Stuffing

2 sweet potatoes

1 tablespoon coconut oil

¼ cup diced white onion

4 ounces white mushrooms, chopped

1 cup Slow Cooker Versatile Seitan Balls, chopped (page 279)

¼ teaspoon ground cumin

¼ teaspoon onion powder

¼ teaspoon salt

Pinch of ground black pepper

Tahini Sauce

¼ cup tahini

1 tablespoon maple syrup

1 tablespoon lemon juice

1 clove garlic

¼ teaspoon salt

Pinch of ground black pepper

INSTRUCTIONS:

Sweet Potatoes and Stuffing

1. Preheat the oven to 350°F.

2. Place the sweet potatoes in the preheated oven and bake for 40 to 45 minutes or until they are soft.

3. Meanwhile, add the oil to a large skillet and heat over medium-high heat. Add the onion and mushrooms and sauté for 10 minutes. Add seitan, cumin, onion powder, salt, and pepper and cook for another 5 minutes. Set aside.

4. Cut the top off the long side of the sweet potatoes and scoop out the centers as best you can. Place the centers in a medium bowl. Add all but ⅓ cup of the seitan-mushroom mixture from the skillet into the bowl. Mix well. Stuff the sweet potato mixture back into the shells. Place back in the oven at 350°F to heat through for 15 minutes.

Tahini Sauce

5. During this time, mix all the tahini sauce ingredients together with 3 tablespoons water. Set aside.

Assembly

6. Remove the potatoes from oven and place on a serving dish. Drizzle tahini sauce over the stuffed sweet potatoes and sprinkle the remaining seitan-mushroom mixture over the top.

Protein: 34 grams per serving
Active Time: 20 minutes
Cook Time: 1 hour
Total Time: 1 hour 20 minutes

CHICKPEA SEITAN FRIED RICE

YIELD: 2 SERVINGS

You won't break a sweat over this recipe. A little bit of preparation and heating in a skillet brings all the flavors together in no time.

INGREDIENTS:

1   cup jasmine rice

1   cup Pressure Cooker Tender Patties (page 286)

1   15-ounce can chickpeas, drained and rinsed

3   tablespoons tamari

3   tablespoons maple syrup

¼   teaspoon ground ginger

2   tablespoons coconut oil

2   carrots, peeled and diced small

1   clove garlic, minced

Green onions, sliced, for garnish

INSTRUCTIONS:

1. Add the rice to a medium saucepan and add 2 cups water. Bring to a boil, cover, turn down the heat to low, and cook for 20 minutes or until the water is absorbed and the rice is tender. Set aside.

2. Place the seitan in a food processor and pulse a few times to make small pieces. Transfer to a small bowl.

3. Add the chickpeas to the food processor and pulse them to make small pieces, about three or four pulses.

4. Mix the tamari, maple syrup, and ginger in a small bowl and set aside.

5. In a large skillet, add the oil and heat over medium-high heat. Add the carrots and fry, flipping with a spatula, for about 5 to 10 minutes. Turn down the heat if necessary to keep the carrots from burning. Add the garlic and stir; cook for 1 minute. Add the rice, prepared chickpeas, and seitan and continue to sauté until there is some browning on the seitan. Add the sauce mixture and continue stirring and flipping with a spatula to incorporate all the sauce and to slightly cook it.

6. Serve garnished with the sliced green onions.

Protein: 40 grams per serving
Active Time: 15 minutes
Cook Time: 15 minutes
Total Time: 30 minutes

PROTEIN POTLUCK SPECIAL

YIELD: 8 SERVINGS

Comfort food for the whole party! Whether for your family or made as a dish to go, this high-protein meal is the whole package.

INGREDIENTS:

- 1 pound lentils
- 1 bay leaf
- 1 tablespoon extra virgin olive oil
- 1 cup finely chopped onion
- 1 green bell pepper, diced
- 2 carrots, finely chopped
- 3 Roma tomatoes, diced
- 1 teaspoon paprika
- 1 teaspoon ground cumin
- ½ teaspoon garlic powder
- ½ teaspoon onion powder
- 1 teaspoon coconut sugar
- ½ teaspoon salt
- 2 Slow Cooker Versatile Seitan Balls, cubed (page 279)

INSTRUCTIONS:

1. Place the lentils and bay leaf in a large saucepan and cook according to package directions.

2. While the lentils are cooking, heat the oil over medium-high heat in a very large skillet. Add the onions and bell pepper and sauté for 10 minutes. Add the remaining ingredients and sauté for 5 minutes. Add the lentils, stir, and cook for 5 minutes to heat through.

Protein: 36 grams per serving
Active Time: 10 minutes
Cook Time: 25 minutes
Total Time: 35 minutes

SLOW COOKER BLACK BEAN AND LENTIL SUPER BURRITOS

YIELD: 6 SERVINGS

These super easy burritos are spicy with lots of texture. The addition of avocados and black olives makes for a hearty meal.

INGREDIENTS:

2   15-ounce cans diced tomatoes

¼   cup salsa

2   15-ounce cans black beans, drained and rinsed

1   cup brown rice

½   cup corn, fresh, frozen, or canned

2   tablespoons taco seasoning

1   teaspoon ground cumin

1   teaspoon salt

2   chipotle peppers in adobo sauce, finely chopped

2½ cups vegetable broth

½   cup lentils

12 whole wheat tortillas

Additional toppings, such as more salsa, avocado or guacamole, and black olives

INSTRUCTIONS:

1. Add the tomatoes, salsa, beans, rice, corn, taco seasoning, cumin, salt, chipotles, and broth to a slow cooker. Stir and cover. Cook on low for 6 to 8 hours or on high for 3 to 4 hours.

2. Add the lentils for the last 40 minutes of cooking. Continue cooking until the lentils are tender. The rice will be tender and most of the liquid will be absorbed. This is the filling.

3. Lay out the tortillas and place about ⅓ to ½ cup (for a very large burrito) of the filling on each tortilla. Spread the filling down through the center of the tortilla. Fold each end about 1½ inches over the point edge of the beans. Then roll up the tortilla along the long edge. If you have a certain technique that you want to use on these, go right ahead.

4. Stack up and serve with more salsa, avocado or guacamole, and black olives.

Protein: 21 grams per serving (2 burritos)
Active Time: 15 minutes
Cook Time: 8 hours
Total Time: 8 hours 15 minutes

LOADED SWEET POTATO BURRITOS

YIELD: 6 SERVINGS

The spicy and sweet contrast in these burritos really hits the spot. This is an updated classic, and you can fill up your tortillas as full as you like.

INGREDIENTS:

1   tablespoon coconut oil

1   sweet potato, peeled and diced

8   ounces mushrooms, sliced

¾   cup diced red onion

¾   cup diced red bell pepper

1½ cups Steamed Seitan Smoky Nuggets (page 283)

1½ teaspoons chili powder

½   teaspoon garlic powder

¼   teaspoon ground cumin

2   cups baby spinach, torn small

6   whole wheat or sprouted grain tortillas

INSTRUCTIONS:

1. Heat the oil in a large skillet over medium-high heat. Add the sweet potato, mushrooms, onion, and bell pepper. Sauté for 15 minutes. Add the seitan, chili powder, garlic powder, and cumin, and cook for 5 more minutes. Add the spinach and cook just a minute or so until wilted.

2. If the tortillas are stiff, such as sprouted grain, then you can warm them in a microwave for 10 to 15 seconds. This will make them easier to roll.

3. Spoon about 1 cup of sweet potato mixture down the center of each tortilla. Roll up. Cut in half for easier handling.

Protein: 19 grams per serving
Active Time: 15 minutes
Cook Time: 20 minutes
Total Time: 35 minutes

SEITAN NUGGETS ROTELLE

YIELD: 6 SERVINGS

It's always a good thing when you can get a family meal on the table in under 30 minutes, especially when you're serving comfort food to the max.

INGREDIENTS:

3 cups rotelle pasta

1 tablespoon extra virgin olive oil

½ cup chopped onion

2 cups Steamed Seitan Smoky Nuggets (page 283), cut into bite-size pieces if necessary

2 cloves garlic, finely chopped

1 15-ounce can diced tomatoes

½ teaspoon Italian seasoning

½ teaspoon salt

¼ teaspoon ground black pepper

Scallions, for garnish (optional)

INSTRUCTIONS:

1. Cook rotelle according to directions on the package.

2. Meanwhile, heat the oil in a large skillet over medium-high heat. Add the onion and seitan and sauté for 10 minutes until the onion is translucent. Add the garlic and cook for another minute. Add the diced tomatoes, Italian seasoning, salt, and pepper. Raise to a boil and then turn down and simmer for 5 minutes. Add the cooked rotelle. Heat through for 5 minutes.

3. If you'd like, garnish with the scallions.

Protein: 20 grams per serving
Active Time: 10 minutes
Cook Time: 20 minutes
Total Time: 30 minutes

BROCCOLI STIR-FRY WITH SEITAN AND CASHEWS

YIELD: 2 SERVINGS

A sweet and tangy sauce combined with veggies and cashews makes this an impressive dish. Serve over sticky jasmine rice for the perfect finish.

INGREDIENTS:

1   cup jasmine rice

2   cups broccoli, stems peeled and diced, florets cut into bite-size pieces

½   cup tamari

2   tablespoons rice vinegar

2   tablespoons maple syrup

½   teaspoon ground ginger

¼   teaspoon garlic powder

1   red bell pepper, diced

2   tablespoons cornstarch or potato starch

¾   cup Pressure Cooker Thai Nuggets (page 288)

½   cup raw cashews

INSTRUCTIONS:

1. Add the rice to a medium saucepan and add 2 cups water. Bring to a boil, cover, turn down heat to low, and cook for 20 minutes or until water is absorbed and rice is tender.

2. Meanwhile, add water to a medium saucepan with a steamer insert and bring to a boil. Add the broccoli to the insert and steam over boiling water for 5 minutes. Remove from steamer and set aside.

3. In a small bowl, mix together the tamari, ¼ cup plus 2 tablespoons water, vinegar, syrup, ginger, and garlic powder.

4. Add 1 tablespoon sauce mixture to a large skillet. Turn the heat up to medium high and add bell peppers. Sauté for 5 minutes. Add the broccoli and cook for 5 minutes. Push the vegetables to the side and add cornstarch to the liquid. Leaving on medium-high heat, stir for 1 minute. Mix all together and add seitan nuggets and cashews. Cook to heat through for about 3 minutes.

5. Serve over the jasmine rice.

Protein: 43 grams per serving
Active Time: 10 minutes
Cook Time: 20 minutes
Total Time: 30 minutes

WHITE BEAN STEW
WITH CHIPOTLE LINKS

YIELD: 6 SERVINGS

This stew is an all-time favorite. It has fresh carrots and corn off the cob, and the plant-based chipotle links give it a sensational taste and texture.

INGREDIENTS:

1 pound navy beans

1 cup Steamed Seitan Chipotle Links (page 284)

2 tablespoons extra virgin olive oil

½ cup diced onion

2 carrots, peeled and chopped

2 cloves garlic, finely diced

2 15-ounce cans fire-roasted tomatoes

2 cobs of corn, kernels cut from the cob

1 cup vegetable broth

1 teaspoon basil

1 teaspoon hot sauce, such as Tabasco (omit if you don't like spicy; you can put it on the table instead)

Protein: 27 grams per serving
Active Time: 15 minutes
Soaking Time: 8 hours
Cook Time: 2 hours 20 minutes
Total Time: 10 hours 35 minutes

INSTRUCTIONS:

The Night Before Cooking

1. Put the beans in a large pot and cover with water. Swish your hand around in the water and pick out any beans that float or don't look good. Drain the beans. Put the beans back into the large pot. Cover with water by about 4 inches above the beans. Let soak on the counter overnight.

The Next Day

2. Drain the beans and cover with 2 to 3 inches of fresh water. Cover and bring to a boil. Turn down the heat to medium low and simmer, partially covered, for about 1½ to 2 hours. Stir a couple of times during cooking time but make sure the temperature stays at a good simmer and the beans are covered with water. The beans are finished when you can squish one with your fingers.

3. When the beans are almost done, brown the seitan links on all sides. Remove from the pan and cut into about ¾-inch pieces.

4. Add the oil to a large skillet and heat to medium low. Add the chopped onion and carrots and sauté for 10 minutes. Add the garlic and cook for 1 more minute.

To Finish

5. Drain the beans and return to the large pot. Add the tomatoes and cook for 10 minutes. It will be soupy. Add the corn, broth, basil, and hot sauce and bring to a boil. Turn down the heat and simmer another 10 minutes.

FRIED HOISIN TOFU WITH PEANUT SAUCE-TOUCHED UDON

YIELD: 2 SERVINGS

The marinated tofu is treated so well in this recipe—lightly crisp on the outside and tender on the inside. If you've never had udon noodles, then now's your chance.

INGREDIENTS:

½ cup hoisin sauce

4 tablespoons soy sauce, divided

4 ounces extra-firm tofu, drained, pressed (page 17), and cubed

¼ cup cornstarch or potato starch

2 tablespoons coconut oil

7 ounces packaged organic udon noodles

½ cup plus 2 tablespoons vegetable broth

¼ cup peanut butter

5 ounces baby spinach

INSTRUCTIONS:

1. Mix the hoisin and 2 tablespoons soy sauce in a small bowl. Add the cubed tofu, toss, and let marinate for 30 minutes.

2. Place the cornstarch on a large plate. Remove the tofu from marinade and lay out on cornstarch, tossing to coat all sides.

3. Heat the oil over medium-high heat in a large skillet. Add the tofu to the hot oil and fry on all sides. Set aside.

4. Fill a large saucepan with water and cover. Bring to a boil and add the udon. Cook for 5 minutes and drain. Set aside.

5. Add the broth and peanut butter to the same saucepan and bring to a boil. Turn down the heat and cook for 2 minutes, then add the udon back into the pan. Coat the udon with the sauce. Add the spinach to the pot and stir into the sauce and noodles. Continue cooking, on low, for about 3 minutes until the spinach wilts.

6. Remove from the heat and divide between two bowls. Place half of the tofu on top of each bowl of udon. Drizzle the remaining hoisin mixture over the top.

Protein: 33 grams per serving
Active Time: 20 minutes
Marinating Time: 30 minutes
Cook Time: 15 minutes
Total Time: 1 hour 5 minutes

ACADIAN BLACK BEANS AND RICE

YIELD: 6 SERVINGS

Here's an updated version of that Southern classic, red beans and rice. This version is made with a variety of spices popular in Cajun country.

INGREDIENTS:

1½ cups brown rice

3½ cups low sodium vegetable broth

1   tablespoon extra virgin olive oil

½   yellow onion, chopped

1   green bell pepper, chopped

2   15-ounce cans black beans, drained and rinsed

1   clove garlic, finely chopped

¼   cup diced tomatoes

1   teaspoon parsley

1   teaspoon garlic powder

1   teaspoon onion powder

1   teaspoon thyme

1   teaspoon oregano

½   teaspoon cayenne pepper

¼   teaspoon ground black pepper

1   teaspoon salt

INSTRUCTIONS:

1. Cook the brown rice by any method you choose. I use a rice cooker. Cook the rice with vegetable broth for this recipe.

2. In a large skillet, heat the oil to medium and then add the onion and bell pepper. Sauté until the onion becomes transparent, about 10 minutes. Add all the remaining ingredients (except the rice) to the large skillet with the onion and bell pepper. Cook for 10 minutes. Add the rice and heat through.

Protein: 16 grams per serving
Active Time: 5 minutes
Cook Time: 40 minutes
Total Time: 45 minutes

CHAPTER SIX

LET'S MAKE SEITAN

SLOW COOKER MAPLE BREAKFAST LINKS

YIELD: 4 CUPS OR 32 SMALL LINKS

These tender and sweet links can be sliced for multiple recipes. Freeze the seitan for a quick meal anytime. Pictured in Seitan Links Tofu Scramble (page 98).

INGREDIENTS:

2 cups vegetable broth

1½ cups vital wheat gluten

½ cup chickpea flour

2 teaspoons ground sage, divided

¼ teaspoon onion powder

¼ teaspoon garlic powder

1 teaspoon salt

¼ cup tomato sauce

2 tablespoons maple syrup

2 tablespoons ketchup

1 teaspoon coconut oil

INSTRUCTIONS:

1. Put the broth and 2 cups water in slow cooker. Turn to low. Add the gluten, flour, sage, onion powder, garlic powder, and salt to a large bowl. Mix well.

2. In a separate small bowl, add ½ cup water, tomato sauce, maple syrup, ketchup, and oil. Mix well.

3. Make a well in the center of the dry mixture and pour in the tomato sauce mixture. Start to stir. This comes together quickly. Squeeze in one hand and let it go through your fingers about 10 times. Start to knead in the bowl. It is a wet mixture but will start to become elastic. Knead for about 3 minutes for a softer and tender breakfast link. The longer you knead, the more elastic it becomes. I keep it all in the bowl for kneading. It is much easier to clean up.

4. Pinch off small chunks and then roll between the palms of your hands, pretty quickly, back and forth. This will make thirty-two small links. You really can't form pretty links, but they will work fine in any recipe you make. Alternatively, you can make fifteen larger links. The larger size would change each link to 15 grams protein.

5. Place the links in the liquid in the slow cooker. Cover and cook on low for 6 hours. They will grow in size as they cook.

6. Remove from the slow cooker and let cool. Refrigerate for up to 5 days and use as needed. They freeze really well, with or without their liquid.

Protein: 22½ grams per serving (3 links)
Slow Cooker Size: 6 quarts
Active Time: 20 minutes
Cook Time: 6 hours
Total Time: 6 hours 20 minutes

SLOW COOKER VERSATILE SEITAN BALLS

YIELD: 3 CUPS OR 34 BALLS

These little round balls add so much flavor and texture to your hardy dishes. They make a fantastic foundation for marinara sauce submarine sandwiches, too. Pictured in Slow Cooker Seitan Bourguignon (page 226).

INGREDIENTS:

1½ cups vital wheat gluten

½   cup chickpea flour

1   tablespoon mushroom powder

½   teaspoon dried oregano

½   teaspoon onion powder

¼   teaspoon garlic powder

¼   teaspoon nutmeg

¼   teaspoon ground ginger

¼   teaspoon ground cloves

¼   teaspoon ground sage

½   teaspoon salt

½   cup tomato sauce, divided

1   teaspoon liquid smoke

1½ cups vegetable broth, divided

Protein: 30 grams per serving (½ cup)
Slow Cooker Size: 6 quarts
Active Time: 15 minutes
Cook Time: 6 hours
Total Time: 6 hours 15 minutes

INSTRUCTIONS:

1. Mix the gluten, flour, mushroom powder, oregano, onion and garlic powders, nutmeg, ginger, cloves, sage, and salt in a large bowl.

2. In a small bowl, add ¼ cup tomato sauce, ¼ cup water, liquid smoke, and ½ cup vegetable broth. Mix well.

3. Make a well in the center of the dry ingredients and pour in the tomato sauce mixture. Mix well and start to knead. Knead for 1 minute or until the dough becomes mildly elastic. You will see the dough slightly pull back as you are kneading and it will be a bit sticky. Pour remaining ¼ cup tomato sauce, 1 cup vegetable broth, and 3 cups water into the slow cooker. Stir.

4. Tear off small chunks of the dough, squeeze into a round shape, and drop into the liquid in the slow cooker. There will be forty-four balls. You can also make seventeen larger balls and cut them after cooking and cooling. Or make two logs and cut into desired shapes. Cover and cook on low for 4 to 6 hours. They will grow in size as they cook. Check at 4 hours and see if you like the texture. They will become firmer as they sit in the refrigerator.

5. Remove from the pot and let cool. Store in the refrigerator for up to 5 days or freeze for up to 4 months.

SLOW COOKER LOG FOR THIN SLICES AND CRUMBLES

YIELD: 4 SERVINGS

One large oval log is a perfect shape for slicing. You have the option of cutting the log into nuggets or you can crumble it. This versatility makes this seitan a go-to for a multitude of recipes. Pictured in Seitan Sloppy Joes (page 145).

INGREDIENTS:

1¼ cups vital wheat gluten

¼ cup chickpea flour

1 tablespoon mushroom powder

2 tablespoon nutritional yeast

½ teaspoon ground sage

½ teaspoon salt

¼ teaspoon garlic powder

¼ teaspoon onion powder

¾ cup tomato sauce

1 tablespoon tomato paste

2 cups vegetable broth

¼ cup tomato sauce

INSTRUCTIONS:

1. Add the gluten, flour, mushroom powder, nutritional yeast, sage, salt, and garlic and onion powders to a large bowl.

2. Mix tomato sauce, tomato paste, and ¼ cup plus 1 tablespoon water in a small bowl. Pour the wet mixture into the dry ingredients.

3. Mix and then knead for about 2 to 3 minutes or until mildly elastic. You will see the dough slightly pull back as you are kneading and it will be a bit sticky. Shape the seitan into a log.

4. Pour 1 cup water, the vegetable broth, and tomato sauce into a 2½- to 3-quart slow cooker. Place the log in the slow cooker or roll loosely in cheesecloth and tie each end with cotton string. It does expand when cooking, so you shouldn't roll it tight. If you don't care that the outside is a bit lumpier after being cooked, then don't bother to roll in cheesecloth. Cover slow cooker and turn to low. Cook on low for 6 hours.

5. Remove the log from the liquid and place aside to cool. Store in the refrigerator for up to 5 days. It can also be frozen for 4 months.

Protein: 31 grams per serving (½ cup)
Active Time: 10 minutes
Cook Time: 6 hours
Total Time: 6 hours 10 minutes

STEAMED SEITAN SMOKY NUGGETS

YIELD: 4 SERVINGS

These smoky, savory bites make for a flavorful addition to an endless number of recipes. Robust in flavor, this small-batch recipe is also great when used as a sandwich filler. This is a densly textured seitan. Pictured in Seitan Nuggets Rotelle (page 264).

INGREDIENTS:

- ¾ cup vital wheat gluten
- ¼ cup plus 2 tablespoons chickpea flour
- 2 teaspoons garlic powder
- 2 teaspoons onion powder
- ½ cup vegetable broth
- 2 tablespoons tomato sauce
- 1 tablespoon tamari
- 1 teaspoon liquid smoke
- ½ teaspoon coconut oil

INSTRUCTIONS:

1. Add the gluten, flour, and garlic and onion powders to a large bowl.

2. Add the broth, tomato sauce, tamari, liquid smoke, and oil to a small bowl and mix well. Pour the liquid into the dry ingredients and mix. Knead for 2 minutes until elastic. You will see it pull back into a rounder shape as you knead. This is a firm dough and will not double in size while cooking.

3. Add 5 cups water to a saucepan. Bring to a boil. Place a steamer basket inside the pan and turn down the heat to simmer.

4. Use a pastry cutter to slice off irregular pieces. You can squeeze them into a ball, as best you can, or leave chunky. You can also steam as one log and cut into chunks after steaming and cooling.

5. Steam for 40 minutes.

6. Remove the seitan to cool and store in the refrigerator for up to 5 days or in the freezer for up to 4 months.

Protein: 30 grams per serving (½ cup)
Active Time: 10 minutes
Cook Time: 40 minutes
Total Time: 50 minutes

STEAMED SEITAN CHIPOTLE LINKS

YIELD: 1 CUP OR 4 LINKS

These spicy hot links can be fried and served as a link, or they can be sliced or crumbled. Regardless, they push so many recipes over the top. This is a small-batch recipe, so you can double the ingredients if you're looking for a larger quantity. Pictured in White Bean Stew with Chipotle Links (page 268).

INGREDIENTS:

- ⅓ cup plus 2 tablespoons vital wheat gluten
- 2 tablespoons chickpea flour
- 1 teaspoon garlic powder
- 1 teaspoon onion powder
- 1 teaspoon taco seasoning
- 2 tablespoons tomato sauce
- 1 teaspoon chipotle hot sauce

INSTRUCTIONS:

1. Add the gluten, flour, garlic and onion powders, and taco seasoning to a large bowl.

2. Mix ¼ cup water, the tomato sauce, and hot sauce in a small bowl and mix well. Pour the liquid mixture into the dry ingredients and mix. Knead for 2 minutes until elastic. You will see it pull back into a rounder shape as you knead. This is a firm dough and will not double in size as cooking.

3. Cut into four equal pieces and roll each one into a log shape.

4. Add 5 cups water to a saucepan. Bring to a boil. Place a steamer basket inside the pan and turn down the heat. Add seitan links to the steamer basket and cover. Steam for 40 minutes.

5. Remove the seitan to cool and store in the refrigerator for up to 5 days or in the freezer for up to 4 months.

Protein: 30 grams per serving (½ cup)
Active Time: 15 minutes
Cook Time: 40 minutes
Total Time: 55 minutes

PRESSURE COOKER TENDER PATTIES

YIELD: 2 CUPS

These patties are ready in no time with an electric pressure cooker and are super simple to make. There seems to be an infinite number of recipe possibilities for these little disks. Pictured in Polenta with Rich Mushroom Gravy (page 239).

INGREDIENTS:

¾ cup vital wheat gluten

¼ cup chickpea flour

2 tablespoons nutritional yeast

½ teaspoon dried basil

½ teaspoon salt

½ teaspoon poultry seasoning

¼ teaspoon garlic powder

¼ teaspoon onion powder

¼ teaspoon paprika

2¼ cups vegetable broth, divided

1 teaspoon extra virgin olive oil

½ teaspoon tamari

2 tablespoons tomato sauce

INSTRUCTIONS:

1. Add the gluten, flour, nutritional yeast, basil, salt, poultry seasoning, garlic and onion powders, and paprika to a large bowl.

2. Mix ¾ cup vegetable broth, oil, and tamari in a small bowl. Pour the wet mixture into the dry ingredients.

3. Mix and then knead for about 2 to 3 minutes or until elastic. It should be stretchy and pull back but still pliable. Divide the dough into eight pieces. Use your fingers to squeeze and work around into a patty measuring about 3 to 4 inches in diameter.

4. Place in an electric pressure cooker.

5. Add 1½ cups water, 1½ cups vegetable broth, and the tomato sauce to a small bowl, stir, and then pour over the seitan cutlets in the pressure cooker. Close the lid, making sure the top knob is turned to sealing. Press Manual on the front of the pot. Push button to 4 (meaning 4 minutes). In a few seconds, the pressure cooker will make a click and start to build pressure. It will take about 15 minutes to build pressure and cook. Leave the cutlets in the pot to set. They will cook more as the pressure is naturally releasing. Don't vent.

Protein: 30 grams per serving (½ cup)
Active Time: 10 minutes
Cook Time: 5 minutes
Rest Time: 1 hour
Total Time: 1 hour 15 minutes

6. After about an hour, go ahead and vent. It may already have cooled completely, but vent to make sure all of the pressure has been released and then open the lid.

7. Remove the cutlets from the liquid and set aside to cool. You can eat them right away, add to a recipe, or keep in the fridge overnight. They are great the next day and keep well in the freezer.

PRESSURE COOKER THAI NUGGETS

YIELD: 4 SERVINGS

Small unformed nuggets with delectable flavors come from your pressure cooker with this recipe. They have an Asian flair and can be added to just about any recipe. Pictured in Broccoli Stir-Fry with Seitan and Cashews (page 267).

INGREDIENTS:

- ¾ cup plus 3 tablespoons vital wheat gluten
- ¼ cup chickpea flour
- ½ teaspoon ground ginger
- ½ teaspoon salt
- ¼ teaspoon garlic powder
- ¼ teaspoon paprika
- ¾ cup vegetable broth
- 2 teaspoons tamari, divided
- 4 teaspoons red curry paste, divided
- 1½ cups vegetable broth, divided

Protein: 30 grams per serving (½ cup)
Active Time: 10 minutes
Cook Time: 5 minutes
Rest Time: 1 hour
Total Time: 1 hour 15 minutes

INSTRUCTIONS:

1. Add the gluten, flour, ginger, salt, garlic powder, and paprika to a large bowl.

2. Mix ¾ cup vegetable broth, 1 teaspoon tamari, and 2 teaspoons red curry paste in a small bowl. Pour the wet mixture into the dry ingredients.

3. Mix and then knead for about 2 to 3 minutes or until elastic. It's a very wet dough but you will see it is still elastic. It should be mildly stretchy and pull back but still pliable. Pinch off pieces of seitan dough into very small balls, about 1 to 1½ inches in diameter. They will fatten up when cooking.

4. Place in an electric pressure cooker.

5. Add 1½ cups vegetable broth, 1½ cups water, and 2 teaspoons red curry paste to a bowl and stir well. Pour over the nuggets in the pressure cooker. Close the lid, make sure the top knob is turned to sealing. Press Manual on the front of the pot. Push button to 4 (meaning 4 minutes). The pressure cooker will make a click and start to build pressure. It will take about 15 minutes to build pressure and cook. Leave the nuggets in the pot to set. They will cook more as the pressure is naturally releasing. Don't vent.

6. After about an hour, go ahead and vent. It may already have cooled completely, but vent to make sure the pressure has released and then open the lid.

7. Remove the nuggets from the liquid and set aside to cool. You can eat them right away, add to a recipe, or keep in the fridge overnight. They are great the next day. You can also freeze them.